First World War
and Army of Occupation
War Diary
France, Belgium and Germany

5 CAVALRY DIVISION
Divisional Troops
Royal Army Service Corps
Divisional Supply Column (71 Company A.S.C.)
1 November 1916 - 28 February 1918

WO95/1163/10

The Naval & Military Press Ltd
www.nmarchive.com
Published in association with The National Archives

Published by

The Naval & Military Press Ltd

Unit 10 Ridgewood Industrial Park,

Uckfield, East Sussex,

TN22 5QE England

Tel: +44 (0) 1825 749494

www.naval-military-press.com

www.nmarchive.com

This diary has been reprinted in facsimile from the original. Any imperfections are inevitably reproduced and the quality may fall short of modern type and cartographic standards.

© Crown Copyright
Images reproduced by permission of The National Archives, London, England, 2015.

Contents

Document type	Place/Title	Date From	Date To
Heading	WO95/1163/10		
Heading	5 Can Div Troops Div Supply Column (71 Coy ASC) 1916 Nov 1918 Feb from 2 (Ind) Cav Div Box 1184 to 11 corps Troops		
War Diary	Woincourt	01/11/1916	10/11/1916
War Diary	Mers	11/11/1916	30/11/1916
Heading	War Diary of Supply Column 5th Cavalry Division From 1st December 1916 to 31st December 1916		
War Diary	Mers	01/12/1916	31/12/1916
War Diary	Woincourt	01/11/1916	10/11/1916
War Diary	Mers	11/11/1916	20/03/1917
War Diary	Quevauvillers 17 Kil. S.E. Amiens	21/03/1917	21/03/1917
War Diary	Marcelcave	22/03/1917	22/03/1917
War Diary	Proyart	24/03/1917	02/04/1917
War Diary	Marcelcave	03/04/1917	07/04/1917
War Diary	Proyart	08/04/1917	14/04/1917
War Diary	Herly 1 Kilometre from Nesle	15/04/1917	17/04/1917
War Diary	Herly	18/04/1917	30/04/1917
War Diary	Herly (Somme)	01/05/1917	06/05/1917
War Diary	Herly	07/05/1917	12/05/1917
War Diary	Monchain	13/05/1917	13/05/1917
War Diary	Monchain Nr. Nesle	13/05/1917	15/05/1917
War Diary	Monchain	15/05/1917	21/05/1917
War Diary	Monchy Lagache	22/05/1917	15/07/1917
War Diary	St. Pol	16/07/1917	07/10/1917
War Diary	Watou	08/10/1917	14/10/1917
War Diary	Watou (Belgium)	15/10/1917	15/10/1917
War Diary	Lumbres	16/10/1917	16/10/1917
War Diary	La Loge	17/10/1917	31/10/1917
War Diary	La Loge (near Hesdin)	01/11/1917	09/11/1917
War Diary	La Loge	09/11/1917	10/11/1917
War Diary	Villers-Carbonnel	11/11/1917	11/11/1917
War Diary	Etrepigny Near Peronne	12/11/1917	19/11/1917
War Diary	Sailly-Sallisel	20/11/1917	23/11/1917
War Diary	Proyart	24/11/1917	27/11/1917
War Diary	Estrees-en-Chaussee	28/11/1917	30/11/1917
War Diary	Framerville (near Proyart)	01/12/1917	04/12/1917
War Diary	Framerville	05/12/1917	07/12/1917
War Diary	Bivouacs on La Chapelette-Etrepigny Rana	08/12/1917	10/12/1917
War Diary	La Chapellette	11/12/1917	30/12/1917
War Diary	Estrees-en-Chaussee	31/12/1917	13/01/1918
War Diary	Estrees-en-c	13/01/1918	25/01/1918
War Diary	Estrees-en-Chaussee	26/01/1918	28/01/1918
War Diary	Halloy (Somme)	29/01/1918	31/01/1918
War Diary	Halloy-l-Pernois	31/01/1918	08/02/1918
War Diary	Longpre les Corps-Saints	09/02/1918	17/02/1918
War Diary	Longpre I-C-S	18/02/1918	21/02/1918
War Diary	Longpre les Corps Saints	22/02/1918	28/02/1918

WO 95/1163/10

5 CAV DIV TROOPS

DIV SUPPLY COLUMN
(71 COY ASC)

1916 NOV
~~1917 JAN~~ — 1918 FEB

FROM 2(ND) CAV DIV BOX 1184
TO 11 CORPS TROOPS

Box 892

Box 1163

Army Form C. 2118.

167

5th Con Dine
Supply Column
Vol V

WAR DIARY
or
INTELLIGENCE SUMMARY.
(Erase heading not required.)

Place	Date	Hour	Summary of Events and Information	Remarks and references to Appendices
WOINCOURT	1/7/16		All "A" section lorries returned to camp this morning after delivering rations last night by 5.30 a.m. at mid day "A" section lorries collected blankets, hangups, tents etc from Rec'd at Bgd to Div H.Q. 6/7, Canadian lorries collected blankets etc from Canadian Bgd & Am Park lorries effects for Andrela Bgd. Lorries started for new area round WOINCOURT at 2.0 P.M. arrived in camp after delivery at 8.30 P.M. Eleven "A" Sect lorries drew hay at ABBEVILLE at 4.30, delivered hay to units & arrived at WOINCOURT at 9.0 P.M. B section drew rations at HANGEST at 1.0 P.M. & arrived at WOINCOURT at 7.30 P.M. Route for all lorries AIRAINES, OISEMENT, ST MAXENT, FEUQUIERES. Distance from CAMPS EN AMIENOIS to WOINCOURT about 42 kilometres.	
"	2/7/16		Rain in the morning, fine afterwards. Roads in new Div area fairly good. Rec'd instructions from O.C. A.S.C. to make road map of this area showing roads fit for traffic in one direction only or in both direction.	
"	3/7/16		Fine today. Capt Stoffers & Capt Wrangham inspected roads in morning to see others in the afternoon. Map was completed by evening. Capt W Stoffers left for 1st Can Div Supply Col at CANAPLES at 3.30 P.M. Train arrived at rail head at 7.30 a.m. Rec'd 4 card passes for self, H/Sgt Cycle Cpl Wrangham & Stafford.	

Army Form C. 2118

16B

WAR DIARY
or
INTELLIGENCE SUMMARY.
(Erase heading not required.)

Instructions regarding War Diaries and Intelligence Summaries are contained in F.S. Regs., Part II. and the Staff Manual respectively. Title pages will be prepared in manuscript.

Place	Date	Hour	Summary of Events and Information	Remarks and references to Appendices
WOINCOURT	4/11/16		Q.M.S. Altree not yet returned from leave. He was due back on 2.8.th ult. Completed map of Divi. area roads obtained permission from French authorities to fetch 2 lorry loads of stores from Treport to put in workshop yard.	
"	5/11/16		Church parade at 11.45 P.M. visited MERS and MAREST OUEST with a view to moving into one or the other place. Found the former a good place, the latter useless. C.Q.M.S. Altree returned from leave today, having been held up at SOUTHAMPTON for 8 days. Weather wet in afternoon.	
"	6/11/16		According to instruction from A.A. & Q.M.G. spent all day with interpreter trying to find billets. French Mayor & Commander of Troops in this place made it impossible for me to arrange anything. Reported to A.A. & Q.M.G. 2/Lt ROBERTSON reported here today for duty	
"	7/11/16		A.A. & Q.M.G. visited MERS today to arrange billets for us. Very wet. Train arrived at 1.30 P.M. today.	
"	8/11/16		Visited MERS today with Capt. Whitcombe & interpreter & arranged billets for supply column 2 D.A.C.D. Canadian Cav. Bgd + Amm. Park. Weather moderately fine showers at intervals. Roads in Woincourt good, but those round AIGNEVILLE awful.	

T. 134. Wt. W708-776. 500000. 4/16. Sir J. C. & S.

Army Form C. 2118

WAR DIARY
or
INTELLIGENCE SUMMARY.
(Erase heading not required.)

Instructions regarding War Diaries and Intelligence Summaries are contained in F. S. Regs., Part II. and the Staff Manual respectively. Title pages will be prepared in manuscript.

169

Place	Date	Hour	Summary of Events and Information	Remarks and references to Appendices
MOINCOURT	9/11/16		Weather fine. Nothing of importance to note.	
"	10/11/16		Weather still fine. Sent my interpreter to Amm. Park to assist them to arrange into their billets at MERS. French road inspector came to make enquiries as to what roads we were chiefly using with a view to keeping them in good repair.	
MERS	11/11/16		"A" section lorries & Hd. Qrs. of Column with workshops & stores moved into MERS this afternoon. One section of Canadian Cav. Bgd. supply Column also moved in. Weather dull, no rain. Good standing for lorries obtained in new Place. Distance to MERS fourteen kilometres.	
"	12/11/16		Lieut. Robertson proceeded on 10 days leave this afternoon. Asked O.C. A.S.C. 1st Bussy detachment consts. returns. Reply to effect that we must wait orders from Fourth Army. All digging parties have returned. Fine weather though dull.	
"	13/11/16		Fifteen men arrived from the Base today in relief of 15 H.T. supply men who have been sent back to Base this afternoon. Recd. confidential memo. from D.W.S re winter training etc. Cpl. Milburn has been ordered to Hay = 16 for the bicycle he lost in AMIENS two months ago. Weather dull, sea fog, no rain.	
"	14/11/16		Fine & dry today. Lieut. Thuwch proceeded to 1st Cav. supply Col. to assist in testing	

Army Form C. 2118

WAR DIARY
or
INTELLIGENCE SUMMARY.
(Erase heading not required.)

Instructions regarding War Diaries and Intelligence Summaries are contained in F. S. Regs., Part II. and the Staff Manual respectively. Title pages will be prepared in manuscript.

17.

Place	Date	Hour	Summary of Events and Information	Remarks and references to Appendices
MERS	14/1/16		offers for position as workshop officer. Train with supplies arrived at 10.30 a.m.	
	15/1/16		Weather fine & dry. Drew 15780 f.s. & paid at column. Leave fund $(Totley Sinker)$ rec'd for Capt. G. Vaughan to report to G.H.Q. 1st Echelon office of DQT MONTREUIL at 3 P.M. tomorrow.	
"	16/1/16		Weather still very fine. Frost during the night. Inspector came from G.H.Q. to check chassis numbers of a few lorries which he had shown differently in his books. Investigated damage to roof of barn at TOTLOY done by lorry. The A46. Drew 7.1065 francs from Field Cashier for pay of detachment.	
"	17/1/16		Very cold but dry. 1 B.C.R. & Bussy detachment lorries returned this evening.	
"	18/1/16		Snow fell last night. Very cold & wet - Totley. Shined in evening. Roads kept nice too good to be spoilt by the weather. Leave closed.	
"	19/1/16		Weather fine & mild. Church parade at 11.45 a.m. Two of A section 3 ton lorries were ordered to report at DARGNIES at 2.0 P.M. for purpose of proceeding up the line with new digging party.	
"	20/1/16		Proceeded to BUSSY to investigate any claims against detachment there ought to be. Found everything had been left correct & there were no claims of any kind	

WAR DIARY
or
INTELLIGENCE SUMMARY.
(Erase heading not required.)

Army Form C. 2118

Place	Date	Hour	Summary of Events and Information	Remarks and references to Appendices
MERS	21/11/16		Received new censor stamps & destroyed old ones. No. 1375. Weather still fine & mild. O.C. proceeded to Base at Rouen today to check company records.	
"	22/11/16		Weather fine & mild. Pte Pheasant returned to Etrunn today after 6 months hard labor. This man should be in an asylum. A charabanc in a very dilapidated condition arrived from Can-Corps Troops Supply Column today. It has been attached to "B" sect. at Woincourt. No instructions have arrived as to the purpose for which it is intended.	
"	23/11/16		Four other ranks proceeded on leave today to England. Weather fine & mild.	
"	24/11/16		Another four men sent on ten days leave this evening. Weather still fine.	
"	25/11/16		Rained all day. Suspected "B" section wells, latrines etc. B section car came into shop for overhaul. "A" section car sent over to Woincourt for temporary replacement.	
"	26/11/16		Nomenclature of supply allotted to 5th Cav Supply Col. Weather wet. Lecture to A sect by medical officer on venereal.	
"	27/11/16		Weather wet all day. Arranged for one musical bath for supply Column & Cam Park. Great inconvenience caused by side car being detached for use of R.E.s.	
"	28/11/16		One hundred men of B section were detailed by the O.C. 10.5.C. in the afternoon to assist in erecting nissen huts by Woincourt railroad for use of horse transport.	

WAR DIARY
or
INTELLIGENCE SUMMARY.
(Erase heading not required.)

Army Form C. 2118

172

Place	Date	Hour	Summary of Events and Information	Remarks and references to Appendices
MERS.	29/1/16		Weather fine & dry. Rec'd men's kit back from field squadron. Weather remained fine but cold & some sea fog. 2/Lt MacTabb's lecture postponed till tomorrow morning as A.C. & B.C. required 60 men to be at Neuil head at 8 a.m. this morning to assist in erecting 7 Nissen huts.	
"	30/1/16		Weather fine. Fifteen Canadian lorries returned to MERS from the section at WINCOURT yesterday, these were being done by horse transport. Four C.B. Daimlers were finished being overhauled by the workshops today. Lieut BECK proceeded on 10 days leave to England this afternoon via HAVRE.	

Ea Rawling Boesay Major
O C 5th Car Supply Co

SERIAL NO. 26.

Confidential
War Diary
of

Supply Column, 5th Cavalry Division.

FROM 1st December 1916. TO 31st December 1916.

(173)

Army Form C. 2118

St Bowdure Sup Col
Vol VI

WAR DIARY
or
INTELLIGENCE SUMMARY.
(Erase heading not required.)

Instructions regarding War Diaries and Intelligence Summaries are contained in F. S. Regs., Part II. and the Staff Manual respectively. Title pages will be prepared in manuscript.

Place	Date	Hour	Summary of Events and Information	Remarks and references to Appendices
MERS	1/1/16		Sent in names of Officers & men desirous of transferring to Heavy Machine Gun Section to-day. Weather cold & wet.	
" "	2/1/16		Still cold & wet. Nothing to report of importance.	
" "	3/1/16		Church parade at 11.45 a.m. by canon Ward. Still cold wet.	
" "	4/1/16		B section moved from WOINCOURT to MERS leaving 6 lorries behind under 2 Lt OWEN. 2 NCOs & 6 men permanently attached to S.W. Btn 8th Fr police duty.	
" "	5/1/16		53 men are detached with chaff cutters, divn police etc. 9 men are at WOINCOURT chiefly supply for work at railhead. 7 men are away with digging party. Lorries the remainder are now at MERS. Weather very windy to SomeWhat wet.	
" "	6/1/16		Sent 8 men to report to O.C. A.S.C. at WOINCOURT for work with Thrashing Machine. Issued instructions re precautions to be taken in case of Zeppelin raids	
" "	7/1/16		Went to see A.D. of S & T with Lt Theisch re new workshop establishment. Weather dull & murky no rain.	
" "	8/1/16		Rec'd new paint for lorries. Capt H. G. Stafford & 6 men proceed on leave to England to-day. Very wet. Roads outside MERS wet & greasy.	

Army Form C. 2118

(174)

WAR DIARY
or
INTELLIGENCE SUMMARY.
(Erase heading not required.)

Place	Date	Hour	Summary of Events and Information	Remarks and references to Appendices
MERS	9/12/16		Rain in morning. Evacuated wolseley car No 1610 in charge of Dvr H²RM to Chépier in car No 725 in charge of 7th A.C.R.	
"	10/12/16		Rec'd letter from A.D.S.T. re standardisation of lorries. Weather fine in morning. Rain in afternoon. Strength of column 443 without Canadians 64 5 units.	
"	11/12/16		4 men reported back from 10th Div²⁸ where they had been used for erecting stolen weather mild, a little rain in afternoon. Painting of lorries was continued.	
"	12/12/16		Inspection by Brig Gen Seely of the supply columns & Amn Park at 11.45 a.m. He was very pleased with everything & said our Wllts were the best of the lot. Rained all day.	
"	13/12/16		13 lorries left there at 7.30 a.m. for GAMACHES to fetch back amn of Sec²bd Bgn who had been digging trenches at the front. lorries had not returned by midnight. Train arrived at GAMACHES at 8.30 a.m. lorries returned to MERS at 12.0 midday. Sent in leave statement to a.s.c. charnp 143 men who have not had leave for over 14 months.	
"	15/12/16		Sent 6 more M.T. men to assist area horse Tpt coy at WOINCOURT in erecting huts. There are now 64 M.T. men detached on various extreme ons duties	

Army Form C. 2118
175

WAR DIARY
or
INTELLIGENCE SUMMARY.
(Erase heading not required.)

Instructions regarding War Diaries and Intelligence
Summaries are contained in F. S. Regs., Part II.
and the Staff Manual respectively. Title pages
will be prepared in manuscript.

Place	Date	Hour	Summary of Events and Information	Remarks and references to Appendices
			besides the detachment of about 100 at WORNCOURT. This leaves 280 men with the	
MERS	16/12/16		Head qrs of the column & companies at MERS. Weather wet nearly all day. It is very difficult to get on with the painting of lorries. Reed notice that G.O.C. will inspect the lorries at 2.30 p.m. next Thursday 21st inst. 2nd Lieut Procter on leave today.	
" "	17/12/16		3 inspectors arrived from G.H.Q. to inspect Form Army. Report was favourable. Weather cold. Delivery of rations by M.T. ceases today. Forwarded detail of establishment in personnel & vehicles of the supply Col to A.D.S.&T. Car Cops.	
" "	18/12/16		Saw letter to Canadian Car B & 2 supply Col saying they were to be stationed in the 5th Car supply Col. Have reed no notification myself. Weather very cold. Church service at 12.0 mid day.	
" "	19/12/16		Orders reed for 10 men & 1 N.C.O to report to R.E. repairing roads at FRIVILLE for work daily at 8.0 a.m. Gave instructions for "A" section to comply tomorrow. Weather very cold.	
" "	20/12/16		Still very cold. Resubmitted suggestion for amalgamation of the two supply Column to A.D of S&T Car Cops through O.C. A.S.C. Held court of enquiry on Canadian supply Column car which was damaged on	

Army Form C. 2118

176

WAR DIARY
or
INTELLIGENCE SUMMARY.
(Erase heading not required.)

Instructions regarding War Diaries and Intelligence
Summaries are contained in F. S. Regs, Part II.
and the Staff Manual respectively. Title pages
will be prepared in manuscript.

Place	Date	Hour	Summary of Events and Information	Remarks and references to Appendices
MERS	21/12/16		in Abbeville on 6th inst, weather still very cold.	
"	22/12/16		Weather much milder. O.C. Div inspected supply column & was extremely satisfied with everything. Capt Warley R.A.M.C went on leave for 14 days this evening.	
"	23/12/16		Still mild. Nothing of importance to report.	
"	24/12/16		Authority was received to draw pebbles from the beach at TREPORT for the Amn H.T Coy at WOINCOURT. Weather cold & wet. Rain all day.	
"	25/12/16		Estimated quantities of oil which supply col could take in & get camels during the next 6 months sent to A.D.g S+T though O.C. A.S.C. Strong wind & rain. Lorries of supply Col arrived by some Amn Park Lorries loaded & delivered so as to relieve the Home Transport. Church service at 9.0 am for supply Col & Amn Parks.	
"	26/12/16		Boxing day. Men had a holiday as far as possible. Weather mild & no wind.	
"	27/12/16		Four lorries commenced running today from MERS to WOINCOURT with stores from TREPORT for the Amn H.T. Coy, two trips per day. Weather still mild.	
"	28/12/16		I saw O.C. Div Re proposed amalgamation of column with Canadian supply column. My suggestion was either to send away Canadians & make up column

Army Form C. 2118.

WAR DIARY
or
INTELLIGENCE SUMMARY.
(Erase heading not required.)

(177)

Place	Date	Hour	Summary of Events and Information	Remarks and references to Appendices
MERS	29/12/16		with entirely British personnel, or attach a section of Canadians to each of my present companies. O.C. A.S.C.'s proposition was to have one British Coy & one Canadian Company. Fine & mild today.	
"	30/12/16		Rec'd permission from A.D. S+T Can Corps to evacuate Canadian Vauxhall car reported damaged on 1/12/16. Weather still wet & mild.	
"	31/12/16		Weather fine. Was informed by War Office that Capt Cahill of Canadian Supply Column having been admitted to hospital is struck off strength of the expeditionary force. Church parade at 11:45 a.m. Weather dull, no rain. Rec'd orders for a lorry to be sent off in relief of digging party lorry at MEAULT. Detailed one of "B" section 3 ton Berna's lorry to be at Amdaba Ht 2 Qrs at 2.0 a.m. tomorrow morning	

Ca Rawlin Bower Major
O C 5th Can Supply Col.

1-1-17

Army Form C. 2118.

(167)

WAR DIARY
or
INTELLIGENCE SUMMARY.
(Erase heading not required.)

Instructions regarding War Diaries and Intelligence Summaries are contained in F.S. Regs., Part II. and the Staff Manual respectively. Title pages will be prepared in manuscript.

Place	Date	Hour	Summary of Events and Information	Remarks and references to Appendices
WOINCOURT	1/7		All "A" section lorries returned to camp this morning after delivering rations last night by 5.30 a.m. at mid day "A" section lorries collected blankets, haversacks, tents etc from medical Bgd to turn H2.6/2, Canadian lorries collected blankets etc from Canadian Bgd. 9 am Park lorries collected for Australian Bgd. Lorries started for new area round WOINCOURT at 2.0 P.M. arrived in camp after delivery at 8.30 P.M. Eleven of "A" sect lorries drew hay at ABBEVILLE at 4.30, delivered hay to units & arrived at WOINCOURT at 9.0 P.M. B section drew rations at HANGEST at 1.0 P.M. & arrived at WOINCOURT at 7.30 P.M. Route for all lorries AIRAINES, OISEMENT, ST MAXENT, FEUQUIERES. Distance from CAMPS EN AMIENOIS to WOINCOURT about 42 kilometres.	
"	2/7		Rain in the morning, fine afterwards. Roads in new area fairly good. Reconnaissance from O.C. A.S.C. to make road map of this area showing roads fit for traffic in one direction only & in both directions.	
"	3/7		Fine today. Capt. Stafford & Capt. Ovingham inspected roads in morning & & were often in the afternoon. Map was completed by evening. Capt. W. Stafford left for 1st Can. Div. Supply Col. at CANAPLES at 3.30 P.M. To-un arrived at rail head at 7.30 a.m. Reed 4 cwt lorries for self, H.Qrs, cyclists & Offrs. O'vingham & Stafford	

T.134. W.L. W708-776. 500000. 4/15. Sir J.C. & S.

Army Form C. 2118.

168

WAR DIARY
or
INTELLIGENCE SUMMARY.
(Erase heading not required.)

Instructions regarding War Diaries and Intelligence Summaries are contained in F. S. Regs., Part II. and the Staff Manual respectively. Title pages will be prepared in manuscript.

Place	Date	Hour	Summary of Events and Information	Remarks and references to Appendices
WOINCOURT	4/11/16		Q.M.S. Altree not yet returned from leave. He was due back on 28th ult: Completed map of Divi area roads. Obtained permission from French authorities to fetch in lorry loads of stores from Treport to put in workshop yard.	
"	5/11/16		Church parade at 11:45 P.M. Visited MERS and MAREST OUEST with a view to moving into one or the other place. Found the former a good place, the latter having been held up at Waless. C.Q.M.S. Altree returned from leave today, having been held up at SOUTHAMPTON for 8 days. Weather wet in afternoon.	
"	6/11/16		Acceding to instruction from A.A. & Q.M.G. spent all day in MERS with interpreter trying to find billets. French mayor & commander of troops in this place made it impossible for me to arrange anything. Reported to A.A. & Q.M.G. 2/Lt ROBERTSON reported for duty today.	
"	7/11/16		AA & QMG visited MERS today to arrange billets for us. Very wet. Train arrived at 12:30 P.M. today.	
"	8/11/16		Visited MERS today with Capt Whitcombe & interpreter & arranged billets for supply Column 2 J.C.B, Coran Town Car Bgd. & Ammn Park. Weather moderately fine showers at intervals. Roads in Woincourt good, but those round AIGNEVILLE are poor.	

T.J.134. Wt. W708—776. 500000. 4/15. Sir J. C. & S.

Army Form C. 2118.

(169)

WAR DIARY
or
INTELLIGENCE SUMMARY.
(Erase heading not required.)

Instructions regarding War Diaries and Intelligence Summaries are contained in F.S. Regs., Part II. and the Staff Manual respectively. Title pages will be prepared in manuscript.

Place	Date	Hour	Summary of Events and Information	Remarks and references to Appendices
WOINPORT	9/6/16		Weather fine. Nothing of importance to note.	
"	10/6/16		Weather still fine. Sent any interpreter to Amm Park to assist them to move into their billets at MERS. French road inspector came to make enquiries as to what roads we were chiefly using, with a view to keeping them in good repair.	
MERS	11/6/16		"A" section lorries & H.Q. of Column with workshops & stores moved into MERS this afternoon. One section of Canadian Cav. Bgd Supply Column also moved in. Weather dull, no rain. Good standing for lorries obtained in Main Place. Distance to MERS fourteen kilometres.	
"	12/6/16		Lieut. Robertson proceeded on 10 days leave this afternoon. Asks O.C. A.S.C. of Bussy detachment could return. Reply to effect that we must wait orders from Fourth Army. All digging parties have returned. Fine weather though dull.	
"	13/6/16		Fifteen men arrived from the Base today in relief of 15 H.T. supply men who have been sent back to Base this afternoon. Recd confidential memo from D.W. re units leaving etc. Cpl. Milburn has been ordered to pay F.16 for the Megale he lost in Amiens two months ago. Weather dull, sea fog, no rain.	
"	14/6/16		Fine & dry today. Lieut Thwench proceeded to 1st Can. Supply Col to assist in Catering	

Army Form C. 2118.

WAR DIARY
or
INTELLIGENCE SUMMARY.
(Erase heading not required.)

Place	Date	Hour	Summary of Events and Information	Remarks and references to Appendices
MERS	15/1/16		officers for positions as washing officers. Train with supplies arrived at 10.30 a.m. Weather fine & dry. Drew 15780 fcs & paid out column. Leave started today. Lorries recd for Capt. G. Vaughan to report to G.H.Q. 1st Echelon the g.D.g.T. MONTREUIL at 3 p.m. tomorrow.	17a
"	16/1/16		Weather still very fine. Frost during the night. Inspector came from G.H.Q. to check charges made of a few lorries which he had shewn differently in his books. Investigated damage to roof of barn at TULLOY done by lorry No A46. Drew 1065 francs from Field Cashier for pay of detachment.	
"	17/1/16		Very cold but dry. 1st BEER & BUSSY detachment lorries returned this evening.	
"	18/1/16		Snow fell last night. Very cold & wet today. Snow in evening. Roads here are too good to be spoilt by the weather. Turned clear.	
"	19/1/16		Weather fine & mild. Church parade at 11.45 a.m. Two g.A. section lorries were ordered to report at BARGNIES at 2.0 P.M. for purpose of proceeding up the line with new digging party.	
"	20/1/16		Proceeded to BUSSY to investigate any claims against detachment there onight. Found everything had been left intact & there were no claims of any kind.	

T.134. Wt. W708-773. 500000. 4/15. Sir J. C. & S.

Army Form C. 2118.

WAR DIARY
or
INTELLIGENCE SUMMARY.
(Erase heading not required.)

(171)

Place	Date	Hour	Summary of Events and Information	Remarks and references to Appendices
MERS	21/11/16		Received new crash stamp & destroyed old one. Weather still fine & mild.	
"	22/11/16		C.Q.M.S. Attrie proceeded to Base at Rouen today to which company records, in extra fine & mild. Pte Pheasant returned to Etrunn today after 6 months hard labour. This man should be in an asylum. A charabanc in a very delapidated condition arrived from Car Coys supply column today. It has been attached to "B" sect at Woincourt. The instructions have arrived as to the purpose for which it is intended. Four other ranks proceeded on leave today to England. Weather fine & mild.	
"	23/11/16		Another four men sent on 10 days leave this evening. Weather still fine.	
"	24/11/16		Rained all day. Inspected "B" section wells, latrines etc. B section car came into shops for overhaul. "A section car sent over to Woincourt for temporary replacement.	
"	25/11/16		Charabanc of supply attd to 5th Cav Supply Col. Weather wet. Ambulance to A sect by medical officer. Again a venereal.	
"	26/11/16		Weather wet all day. Arranged for an avenwijk lathe for supply Column & Canadians. Great inconvenience caused by side car being detached for use of R.E.s.	
"	27/11/16		One hundred men of B section were detailed by the O.C. A.S.C. in the afternoon to proceed in existing convoy lots by Woincourt road back for use of same transport.	

Army Form C. 2118.

172

WAR DIARY
or
INTELLIGENCE SUMMARY.
(Erase heading not required.)

Instructions regarding War Diaries and Intelligence Summaries are contained in F. S. Regs., Part II. and the Staff Manual respectively. Title pages will be prepared in manuscript.

Place	Date	Hour	Summary of Events and Information	Remarks and references to Appendices
Mr B	29/7/16		Weather fine & dry. Received mails back from field squadron.	
"			Weather remained fine but cold. Some sea fog. It was that section returned till tomorrow morning as O.C. A.S.C. required to men to be on unit head at 8 a.m. this morning. Assist in erecting 7 Nissen huts.	
"	30/7/16		Weather fine. Fifteen Canadian lorries returned to M.E.R.s from the section at WINCOURT yesterday, their work being done by horse transport. Four C.B. Daimlers were finished being overhauled by the workshops today. Lieut. BECK proceeded on 10 days leave to England this afternoon via HAVRE.	

Ca Ramsey Brevet Major
O.C. 5th Carr Supply Co

T.J.134. Wt. W708-776. 500000. 4/15. Sir J. C. & S.

Army Form C. 2118.

(173)

WAR DIARY
or
INTELLIGENCE SUMMARY.
(Erase heading not required.)

1916

Instructions regarding War Diaries and Intelligence Summaries are contained in F. S. Regs., Part II. and the Staff Manual respectively. Title pages will be prepared in manuscript.

Place	Date	Hour	Summary of Events and Information	Remarks and references to Appendices
MERS	1/7/16		Sent in names of officers & men desirous of transferring to Heavy Machine Gun Section to day. Weather cold & wet.	
"	2/7/16		Still cold & wet. Nothing of infantry importance.	
"	3/7/16		Church parade at 10.45 a.m. by carmen ward. Still cold wet.	
"	4/7/16		B section moved from WOINCOURT to MERS leaving 6 lorries behind under 2/Lt OWEN, 2 NCOs & 6 men permanently attached to S.W. H.Q. for police duty.	
"	5/7/16		53 men are detached with chaff cutter, Aire julie etc. 6 men are at WOINCOURT chiefly supply for work at railhead. 7 men are away with digging party lorries. The remainder are now at MERS. Weather very windy & showery, but not wet.	
"	6/7/16		Sent 8 men to return to O.C. A.S.C. at WOINCOURT for work with Thackeray Machine. Issued instructions re precautions to be taken in case of Zeppelin raids.	
"	7/7/11		Went to pse A.D.S's & T with Lt Therach re new workshops establishment. Weather dull & windy, no rain.	
"	8/7/16		Rec'd new "paint" for lorries. Capt. H.G. Stafford & 6 men proceeded on leave to England to day. Very wet, parade outside MERS wet & greasy.	

Army Form C. 2118.

(174)

WAR DIARY
or
INTELLIGENCE SUMMARY.
(Erase heading not required.)

Instructions regarding War Diaries and Intelligence Summaries are contained in F. S. Regs., Part II. and the Staff Manual respectively. Title pages will be prepared in manuscript.

Place	Date	Hour	Summary of Events and Information	Remarks and references to Appendices
MERS	9/12/16		Rain in morning. Evacuated Wolseley car No 1610 in charge of Dvr H.Q.M. to Dunkirk lorry car No 725 in charge of 9th L.A.C.B. He is little from A.D of 9 & T re standardisation of lorries. Weather fine in morning. Rain in afternoon. Strength of Column 443 without Canadians 645 with.	
"	10/12/16		4 men reported back from 18th Division where they had been used for erecting shelters. Weather much as of the afternoon. Painting of lorries was continued. Inspection by Brig Gen Sully of the Supply Columns & Amn Park at 11.45 a.m. He was very pleased with everything & said our WOLRS were the best of the lot. Rained all day.	
"	11/12/16		13 lorries left Mers at 7.30 p.m. for CAMACHES to fetch back men of Second Bgd who had been digging trenches at the front. Lorries had not returned by midnight.	
"	12/12/16		Lorries arrived at CAMACHES at 3.30 a.m. Lorries returned to MERS at 12.0 mid day.	
"	13/12/16		Two men on leave statement – to O.C. O.S.C. showing 1143 men who have not had leave for over 14 months.	
"	14/12/16		Sent 6 more M.T. men to assist our horse Tpt Coy at WINCOURT in erecting huts. There are now 14 M.T. men detached on various extraneous duties	

Army Form C. 2118.

175

WAR DIARY
or
INTELLIGENCE SUMMARY.
(Erase heading not required.)

Place	Date	Hour	Summary of Events and Information	Remarks and references to Appendices
MERS	16/12/16		Leaves the detachment of about 100 at WINCOURT. This leaves 280 men with the Hd.qrs of the Column + companies at MERS. Weather wet nearly all day. It is very difficult to get on with the painting of lorries. Recd notice that G.O.C. will inspect the lorries at 2.30 p.m. next Thursday 21st inst. 2 G.S. waggons on June lorry.	
"	17/12/16		9 rural cars arrived from G.H.Q. to inspect Fodder lorry. Report was favourable, weather cold, delivery of rations by M.T. ceases today. Forwarded detail of establishment in personnel + vehicles of the supply Col. to A.D.S+T Corps. Sent letter to Reread War Car B.g.E. supply Col saying they were to be divested in the 5th Corp Aux'fly Col. Have recd no notification myself. Weather very cold. Church service at 12.0. Mud day.	
"	18/12/16		Paraded men for 10 men d 1 N.C.O to report to R.E. repairing roads at FRIVILLE for work daily at 8 a.m. Gave instruction for "A" section to empty tramcars. Weather very cold.	
"	19/12/16		Still very cold. Received suggestion for amalgamation of the two supply Columns to A.D.J.S+T. Corps through O.C. A.S.C.	
"	20/12/16		Held Court of Enquiry on Canadian Supply Column Car which was damaged on	

Army Form C. 2118.

176

WAR DIARY
or
INTELLIGENCE SUMMARY.
(Erase heading not required.)

Place	Date	Hour	Summary of Events and Information	Remarks and references to Appendices
MERS	21/12/16		in Albeville on 6 unit. Weather still very cold.	
"	22/12/16		Weather much milder. G.O.S. Div inspected supply Column & was extremely satisfied with everything. Capt Warley R.A.M.C. went on leave for 14 days this evening.	
"	23/12/16		Still mild. Nothing of importance to report.	
"	24/12/16		Authority was received to draw pebbles from the beach at TREPORT for the area H.T. Coy at WOINCOURT. Weather cold & wet. Rain all day. Estimated quantities of which supply col could take in 4-5 gal loads during the next 6 months sent to A.D.S.&T. though O.C. a.s.c. strong wind & rain.	
"	25/12/16		Lorries of Supply Col assisted by some am Park lorries loaded & delivered as an to relieve the Horse Transport. Church service at 9.0 a.m for supply col & am Parks.	
"	26/12/16		Boxing day. Men had a holiday as far as possible. Weather mild & no wind.	
"	27/12/16		Four lorries commenced running today from MERS to WOINCOURT with stones from TREPORT for the am H.T. coy, two trips per day. Weather still mild.	
"	28/12/16		I saw o.c. re proposed amalgamation of Column with Canadian supply Column. My suggestion was either to send away Canadians & make up Column	

T.J.134. Wt. W708—776. 500000. 4/15. Sir J. C. & S.

Army Form C. 2118.

(177)

WAR DIARY
or
INTELLIGENCE SUMMARY.
(Erase heading not required.)

Instructions regarding War Diaries and Intelligence Summaries are contained in F.S. Regs., Part II. and the Staff Manual respectively. Title pages will be prepared in manuscript.

Place	Date	Hour	Summary of Events and Information	Remarks and references to Appendices
M.F.R.S.	29/12/16		with entirely British personnel, an attack in each section of my present companies O.C. A.S.C. proposition was to have one British Coy & one Canadian company. Fine today & mild.	
"	30/12/16		Recd personnel from A.D.S. & 7 Car. Coys. to reorient Canadian Vauxhall car completed damaged on 15th. Weather still wet & mild. Weather fine. Was informed by War Office that Capt Cahill of Canadian supply column having been admitted to hospital is struck off strength of the expeditionary force.	
"	31/12/16		Church parade at 11:45 am. Weather dull. Me Laurin Pte & other prs in Coy to be send off in relief of digging party lay at M.E.A.V.T. Details as of "B" Section 3 Ton French Lorry to be at Amabala H.Q. Cars at 9 am tomorrow morning.	

1-1-17

La Chaustin - Berrey Major
O.C. 5th Can supply Col.

Army Form C. 2118.

178

71 Coy ASC

WAR DIARY
or
INTELLIGENCE SUMMARY.

(Erase heading not required.)

Place	Date	Hour	Summary of Events and Information	Remarks and references to Appendices
MERS	1/1/17		Weather cold. Rec'd instructions re running of post lorry in event of the thaw scheme coming into operation.	
"	2/1/17		Weather still int—dry. Painting of lorries was progressed with.	
"	3/1/17		Rec'd letter from A.D.S+T saying all spiral units & cycles were to be marked V.F. on a blue & white numberplate. Correspondence re C.S.M. Eastman-Weeks answered – returned strong wind interfering with painting of lorries again.	
"	4/1/17		140 good conduct badges awarded to men of the column who have been present for 2 years without an entry (regimental). Strifes have been demanded from the Ordnance. Fine & dry in the afternoon.	
"	5/1/17		Rations for the majority of units of the Div'n were drawn & delivered by the supply column today, & will be for the following 4 days. Weather fine. Arranged for an R.E service in mens church on Sunday next. Sent round new cups & history sheets to the cars for completion.	
"	6/1/17		Major Brawdy Bovey, MSAS. for five days special leave to England. Capt K.W. Morley returned from fourteen days' Special leave to England. The weather turned colder during the night but has been fine all day.	

Army Form C. 2118.

(179)

WAR DIARY
or
INTELLIGENCE SUMMARY.
(Erase heading not required.)

Place	Date	Hour	Summary of Events and Information	Remarks and references to Appendices
MERS	7/4/17		Board of inquiry held by Capt Whitcomb of Ammunition Park at 2 p.m. on bus which received in Lansdowne Brigade Supply Column denial on Friday. Received instructions from G.H.Q. that those had got to be on medical inspection for scabies once a week.	
"	8/4/17		Unit leaving all day, all work had to be stopped in consequence from except these unlies were sent to the sick weather.	
"	9/4/17		Cpl Nield Henry U.S. Urea Horse Transport sick and say that they would not require anymore horses at WOINGOURT for the present. Received orders that the U.S.U.S.M. to continue to Bam-Radon and [illegible] for horses and if & including the 13th inst. that he was to run to M.T. and 2 supply men to be attached to the Horse Transport Company to be [illegible] duty for at least 14 days. 2nd Lieut Blunt returned from [illegible] days General Leave of England. Lapt Birkhead arrived with [illegible] of Gurkhas Justice Drew 13265 francs of [illegible] to pay out to the Echelon unit. Gurkhas still very bad owing of [illegible] to continue punishing the Irish. The new Yellow card passes arrived.	
"	10/4/17		Lorries more ordered to be at Durham by 9 a.m. but were not returned on the Southern to [illegible] until 1 P.M. returning to camp after delivering Indians & troops at 5-30 P.M. Received orders from the U.S.U.S.O. to Shed 3 vehicles to the Rhine House Transport Company, the men long attached to the WOINGOURT detachment and reporting daily for duty to the U.S. H. A.G. Company	
"	12/4/17		Board of inquiry will be [illegible] Capt Boyle Stafford of "B" Section office to enquire into the [illegible]	

Army Form C. 2118.

180

WAR DIARY
or
INTELLIGENCE SUMMARY.
(Erase heading not required.)

Instructions regarding War Diaries and Intelligence Summaries are contained in F.S. Regs., Part II. and the Staff Manual respectively. Title pages will be prepared in manuscript.

Place	Date	Hour	Summary of Events and Information	Remarks and references to Appendices
MERS	12/1/17.		Received by the Brigadier who was Marches than by a First car on the evening of the 8/1/17. Strength of Squen. not including Servants 4 + 6.	
"	13/1/17.		Sent four Lewis Guns & gunners to Chinnah Machine Gun Squadron at FLORIVILLE & Army orders and Rest at Field Squadron to replace one of their drivers sick and granted 14 days leave. Received orders from I.C. 2 M.G. to send five men to V.B. horse dep. at FRIVILLE. the men being selected to fulfil the L.O.4 S.O. 4 in Field Squadron. Forwarded delivery returns and forage & stores for horses. 4 C.B. Reinhardt and Mr/m 1st Cavalry Division under orders from It.D.	
"	14/1/17.		F.9.O.17 through V.C. 1st V.B. for Re-standardization of stores in Brigade depot. Recommended to carry Spares for Vyan front Transport Company. Weather fine but cold. Y Type Receiver attached to 9th Light Squadron to Battery not in for inspection. Hope using next to the 3rd Cavalry Division.	
"	15/1/17.		2nd Lieut Botolwid granted Short leave to ALBERT by I.C. 1st V.B. V.C. and 2nd Lieut Blunt to WOINCOURT to take over 2nd Lieut Botolwids duties whilst on leave. Lieut Mr York use the luck from home on 13th inst has not yet returned reported home at D.C.V.B. Weather mild fine.	
"	16/1/17.		carrying on with funeral of horses. Med B Type Detonator sent to 7th Cavalry Division & one Y Type to the 3 Cavalry Division. Received	

Army Form C. 2118.

WAR DIARY
or
INTELLIGENCE SUMMARY.
(Erase heading not required.)

Place	Date	Hour	Summary of Events and Information	Remarks and references to Appendices
MERS	17th		Mr Deaves lorry from 1st Cavalry Division to went instruction before being handed over to the Left Present Horse Shoff lorries from 1st & 2nd Cavalry Divisions. Weather turned very bad approx. raining & snowing all day.	
"	18/1/17		Major Cauley Browne returned from 10 days leave to England today. 2t MacGrab returned from leave, having had 2 days extension. Weather cold & roads outside Mers very bad for lorries being 3 or 4 inches deep in snow.	
"	19/1/17		3 Leyland lorries arrived from 3rd Cav: Supply Col. Weather very cold but dry.	
"	20/1/17		Weather fine & dry. Numbered Column infantry acct altered to A.S.C 1233.	
"	21/1/17		Lt Gregory granted 3 days leave to Paris to commence on the 26-1-17. Lesson Morel held at 3 pm. Shifted at 11-30. Received orders from the O.C. of D.C. to move 5 miles nearer to the Front Line at FRIVILLE.	
"	22/1/17		Weather very cold but dry. Major Bradley Barry received orders to proceed to III Corps as 2nd in at Moville. He took over command of the Bight Ammunition Park.	
"	23/1/17		Major Bradley Barry handed over 5 Leaveley Supply Column to 2t Capt. W. H. Warper-Vaughan. 2t Williams "A" beam belonged the first demand of the Divisional Supt Amusement starting this Wednesday. R. 3-0.	

WAR DIARY or INTELLIGENCE SUMMARY.

Army Form C. 2118.

(Erase heading not required.)

Place	Date	Hour	Summary of Events and Information	Remarks and references to Appendices
MERS	24/7		Our lorries just out of action. Although the fort Major Beraldy Derry left in the 11. Lorry. Lieut Parrell Marshall now acting B.S.O. for Kinnerdean's Armoury Depot and Schedule.	
"	25/7		On duty in the workshops & W.B. W.D.G. Rec. Stores 12 O.S.O. & Sup. Column with. Lieut Henry proceeds on three days leave to Paris. Lieut Reid returned from Armourers to Supply Depot. Armourers Park Workshops still going with. Lieut Blunt attached 11/3 Landshild Institute.	
"	26/7		On duty in the Supply Train not wiring at Railhead until 8 P.M. 12 lorries had to be met & returned to every Details of Group. Lieut Beck and two N.B. & O. left for a weeks instruction at the two extracts AWLT & R.S. on training a force of lead sump guards returned. The wireless party on board at sea. Hill Journey here.	
"	27/7		Lieut Thwaites left for 10 days general leave to England. And it and 45 lorries to Railhead to every returns & large convoy to the duty record of the supply train. The from Dukra forwarded and returning to the Return gave a show for the Division at the convoy MERS, 7 more lorries out of action. Convoy to the fort.	
"	28/7		Supply train cleared out with stores needed 6 P.M. 30 lorries had to be met & returned & left empty returns & large Machine Well also at Emergency duty.	
"	29/7		Mr Supply Train wiring at Railhead. Lieut Gregory returned from Paris leave. Lt. D of M & T Infantry	

Army Form C. 2118.

5th Cow Divisional
Supply Column
Vol VII

WAR DIARY
or
INTELLIGENCE SUMMARY.

(Erase heading not required.)

Instructions regarding War Diaries and Intelligence Summaries are contained in F. S. Regs., Part II. and the Staff Manual respectively. Title pages will be prepared in manuscript.

Place	Date	Hour	Summary of Events and Information	Remarks and references to Appendices
MERS	30/1/17		Inspected workshops. Four more lorries out of action through frost. The supply train for the 29/1/17 arrived at 7-30 AM. The lorries for 4-day issued at 6-30 PM.	
"	31/1/17		Rations & forage for the division was delivered by lorry. Have been applied for a transfer to Major Bailey's Ammunition Column. Snowed hard during the night but was fine all day. 8.5 tons of rations & forage had to be delivered by lorries.	

1-2-17.

M Wyllarson-Hughes Capt.
O.C. 5th Cavalry Supply Column.

Army Form C. 2118.

WAR DIARY
or
INTELLIGENCE SUMMARY.
(Erase heading not required.)

Instructions regarding War Diaries and Intelligence Summaries are contained in F. S. Regs., Part II. and the Staff Manual respectively. Title pages will be prepared in manuscript.

Place	Date	Hour	Summary of Events and Information	Remarks and references to Appendices
MERS	1/2/17		Received orders from 2/ H.Q. for 2nd Lieut Irwin to be transferred to No 16 Ammunition Sub Park, and for 2/Lieut Blunt of the Park to go to 2nd Canadian Supply Column. Baggage & forage had to be delivered by lorries to the Division. Sent 2 lorries to Corps Head Quarters to be collected for 7 days under orders from M.D. of D.G.T.	
"	2/2/17		Front still continued.	
"	3/2/17		2/Lieut Irwin left for No 16 Ammunition Sub Park. Front still continued.	
"	4/2/17		Major B. E. Pryke assumed to take over command of the Column.	
			Orders Rec'd today to move up Lt (Temp Lt) A. H. Gwynne Vaughan to report to 49 Coy A.S.C. also 2/Lt (Temp Lieut) J.K. M'O. Farrell to 5th Cav Div A.S.C., also Lieut T.A. Hall to Canadian Cav Bde A.S.C. also Lieut T.R. Callender-Young to join 5th Cav Supply Column, also T. Lieut H. Humphries to 5th Cav Supply Col. as Subaltern.	O.o A.E. 5th Cav Div 3/2/17 S.727
"	5/2/17		T. Capt Gwynne Vaughan proceeded to join his new unit as above ordered.	
"	6/2/17		Nil.	
"	8/2/17		16 lorries to DOULLENS for relieving Pioneer Battalion. Major Mayne took over A.D.T.T. Corps H.Q. at REGNIERE ECLUSE	

Army Form C. 2118.

WAR DIARY
or
INTELLIGENCE SUMMARY.
(Erase heading not required.)

Instructions regarding War Diaries and Intelligence Summaries are contained in F. S. Regs., Part II. and the Staff Manual respectively. Title pages will be prepared in manuscript.

Place	Date	Hour	Summary of Events and Information	Remarks and references to Appendices
MERS	8/2/17		re reorganisation of the 3rd & our Div Supply Col	
	9/2/17		Lieut Thenech returned from leave. C of D on frozen radiators & damaged cylinder head.	
	10/2/17		Amalgamated A & B Sections	
	11/2/17		nil	
	12/2/17		nil	
	13/2/17		Transferred 46 men to Amm Park of 5th Can Div. Also 15 Renno lorries. Took over 50 men + 14 Commer lorries from 5th Can Div Amm Park. Medical Inspection for venereal disease in the whole column but I can found.	
	14/2/17		nil	
	15/2/17		Large hill	
	16/2/17		lorries went to railhead WOINCOURT blew up 85 tons	
	17/2/17		5 lorries transport wood to SAIGNEVILLE	

Army Form C. 2118.

WAR DIARY
or
INTELLIGENCE SUMMARY.
(Erase heading not required.)

Instructions regarding War Diaries and Intelligence Summaries are contained in F.S. Regs., Part II. and the Staff Manual respectively. Title pages will be prepared in manuscript.

Place	Date	Hour	Summary of Events and Information	Remarks and references to Appendices
MERS	18/7/17		Major R.L. Magee indisposed. Thunderstorm evening. No lorries to run except for post rations & visit.	
	19/7		Nil	
	20/7		Nil	
	21/7		Routine work	
	22/7		Submitted return of govt. buildings in charge of unit – 5 buildings required at local Mairie.	
	23/7		NISSEN huts – 695. Feeding strength of unit – 695. 40 men to be sent daily for Road. repairing with R.E.s. Local roads in extremely bad condition – very poor foundation.	
	24/7			
	25/7		Lieut. J. Halley lorries to H.Q. Repair shops for overhaul per instruction received from G.H.Q.	
	26/7		Submitted average mileage petrol used for 4 weeks ending 27/7/17. Lorries = 74,008 miles 6765 galls petrol – 85%% galls. – 156 galls. Motorcycles 4810 miles – 85½ galls. Leave party return home. Base after spending 6 weeks here.	

Sir J.C.&S.

Army Form C. 2118.

WAR DIARY
or
INTELLIGENCE SUMMARY.
(Erase heading not required.)

Instructions regarding War Diaries and Intelligence Summaries are contained in F.S. Regs., Part II. and the Staff Manual respectively. Title pages will be prepared in manuscript.

Place	Date	Hour	Summary of Events and Information	Remarks and references to Appendices
MERS	27/7		weather fine — providing 7 lorries for 28 - Mar 1 & 3rd Yrs 5th Aux. Depots LE TREPORT Lt. J.J. Gregory started to Hospital.	
	28/7		weather fine — routine transport.	

July 28th 1917

McMurdwood
Lieut. for
Major
O.C. 5th Aux Supply Column

St. Omer Rouen Sup Col

WAR DIARY
or
INTELLIGENCE SUMMARY.
(Erase heading not required.)

Army Form C. 2118.
Vol IX

Place	Date	Hour	Summary of Events and Information	Remarks and references to Appendices
MERS	1/3/17		Fine - proposal from ADST, had no 2 suggestion from to Gen RAWSON - that all men below the age of 40 be replaced by older men - does not seem practicable in the M.T. head.	
	2/3/17		Fine - NIL	
	3/3/17		Major R.L. Traynor, ASC admitted N°3 General Hospital LE TREPORT T/Capt. H.P. BLACKWOOD. C.A.S.C. arrived temporary command & unit. T/Lieut R.H. BECK. A.S.C. proceeded to join 66th Siege Btty, "P" troops T/2/Lt D.L. BLUNT. A.S.C. to remain with his unit - previous movement order cancelled.	
	4/3/17		Lorries sent only run when provided with special passes issued by O.C. H.Q.	
	5/3/17		Fine - Limited return of ages of men serving in unit. Men under 25 = 162. between 25 & 30 years = 216. between 30/40=161 ” over 40 years = 81	
	6/3/17		hold this June - NIL	

Army Form C. 2118.

WAR DIARY
or
INTELLIGENCE SUMMARY.
(Erase heading not required.)

Instructions regarding War Diaries and Intelligence Summaries are contained in F.S. Regs, Part II. and the Staff Manual respectively. Title pages will be prepared in manuscript.

Place	Date	Hour	Summary of Events and Information	Remarks and references to Appendices
MERS	7/7/17		Very cold – Past Imperial Bishops today – total yrs 11795	
	8/7/17		Cold – snow. provided 18 lorries to convey troops to Mers. trops. Being Imminent on 8th, 9th & 10th.	L.G.O.C. lorries (A.O.527 7/6047) 2/7 8/7
	9/7/17		Cold – slight snow – Received authority to evacuate strength of unit 650 all ranks – gas helmet drill –	
	10/7/17		Fine & mild – C.Q.M.S. GIBBS (Canadian Ctt) placed under close arrest on charge of disposing of Government property.	
	11/7/17		Lieut W Strand admitted Hospital at PARIS (went from front PARIS)	
			Capt REMAYNE invalided to England	
	12/7/17		Inspector from BAO (...) examining & S.B. Daimler engines which have proved unsuccessful were specially dismantled for that purpose. Received orders to be prepared to move.	2/Lt DLBLUNT
	13/7/17		returned from trafalgar. 5 lorries proceeded to DIEPPE for loved ones Dull but fine -	
			cake which was delivered to GAMACHES	
	14/7/17		Fine – 11 lorries proceeded to DIEPPE for lived cake	

Army Form C. 2118.

WAR DIARY
or
INTELLIGENCE SUMMARY.
(Erase heading not required.)

Instructions regarding War Diaries and Intelligence Summaries are contained in F.S. Regs., Part II. and the Staff Manual respectively. Title pages will be prepared in manuscript.

Place	Date	Hour	Summary of Events and Information	Remarks and references to Appendices
MERS	15/3/17		Fine warm - 1 lorry to MERICOURT for R.E.'s Letter from A.D.S.T. stating that Lt. Humphries R.A. is to be the "A" Corps Rly the senior workshop officer	
	16/3/17		Fine - nothing to report	ADST M/153/0/5 11-3-17
	17/3/17		Fine - Lorry No. 4999 returned from detachment with VI Corps (Pioneer party) 1st borrowed round work to loading & delivering stones to the Division. British section loaded today & returned to MERS. WOINCOURT detachment returned All men on detailed work borrowed at MERS reported unit.	
	18/3/17		Dull cold - Indian section ending at 9pm. British section moved out to deliver to units at rear line. between Yonckel from Rees 7d Squadron RE on Der Tournamer 3-0.	
	19/3/17		Cold - "B" sec. delivered AMBALA > SEC'BAD Rds. 1st went Willis - Indian Rds FRMA Rds to SENARPONT Received telephonic orders from the O.C. H.Q. Rly. to be prepared	

WAR DIARY or INTELLIGENCE SUMMARY

Army Form C. 2118.

Place	Date	Hour	Summary of Events and Information	Remarks and references to Appendices
MERS	19/3/17		to move at short notice for (small) Reparations issued this evening to all ranks - also rum ration. Very cold windy - Breakdown lorrie (SS) to Verdun & pick up Aust H.T. lamp at WOINCOURT & deliver to QUEVAUVILLERS (N.E. of POIX).	
	20/3/17		X roads by SENARPONT before delivery today. British lee (lodes) & Nigro Workshops moved to QUEVAUVILLERS at 13 noon. 25 breakdown lee lorries detailed for duty yesterday not returned to MERS at 8 pm - then have to pick up damaged rations, deliver to new billets today, stood at WARFUSEE - ABANCOURT at 1 a.m. tomorrow - stiff march.	
QUEVAUVILLERS 17 kil. S.E. AMIENS	21/3/17		Moved to new billets at MARCEL CAVE at 1-30 pm. Very cold - heavy fall of snow. Pulled limousine LA PLAQUE.	
MARCEL CAVE	22/3/17			
PROYART	24/3/17 cold	Moved to new billets at PROYART - (Pulled at LA PLAQUE) Workshops blacks left behind at MARCELCAVE under instructions from O.H.B. in advanced to other transport on Ambulance. Pulled tomorrow morning to CHUIGNES. Lieut N.H. Stafford still in Hospital at PARIS. (Summer fire)	

Army Form C. 2118.

WAR DIARY
or
INTELLIGENCE SUMMARY.
(Erase heading not required.)

Instructions regarding War Diaries and Intelligence Summaries are contained in F. S. Regs., Part II. and the Staff Manual respectively. Title pages will be prepared in manuscript.

Place	Date	Hour	Summary of Events and Information	Remarks and references to Appendices
PROYART	25/7/17		Coy. but lines – Packed in yesterday – "B" section delivered labels & haversack bless & Iron Troops rations to dump at HEADCOURT and Det'd had Pole to BOIS DE MIRAUMONT huts and N. of PERONNE	
"	26/7/17		Met. hot. mild – "B" Section delivered to some dumps as yesterday. "B" Section loaded & delivered at 5pm. "B" Section lost at CORBIE tomorrow + "B" Section had a road	
"	27/7/17		railhead (CHUIGNES) thro' entire day rations for the T/Lt CALLENDER-YOUNG ceased. Limited to dumps ibtpd with readr. Major. V.M. HUTTON. D.S.O. joined erased around division to the dump at report.	Visit
"	28/7/17		Met – nothing particular to report	
"	29/7/17		Met – "B" Sect. tpt to dump at HERBECOURT – "B" Sec loaded as usual Met – Roads very bad – provided 9 lorries & 1 Bus for use of 39 Div'l HQ at PERONNE – "B" Sec. delivered bread area after dly 19 lorries were to report DHQ. R.E. to carry Div'l laggage bivvie area.	
"	30/7/17		Met – Division moved back known hills around VILLERS-BRETONNEUX – loaded in bulk – rains of cauliflower as vegetable ration.	
"	31/7/17		Weather improving somewhat – Returned 27 supply men & 9 – M.T. surplus details to the Base. Total strength of laborers 611 all ranks	V M HUTTON MAJOR A.S.C. D.S.O. Comdg 5th Div. Train

Army Form C. 2118.

WAR DIARY
or
INTELLIGENCE SUMMARY.
(Erase heading not required.)

Vol 10

5TH CAVALRY SUPPLY COLUMN.

Place	Date	Hour	Summary of Events and Information	Remarks and references to Appendices
PROYART	1/7/7		Chavery - loading and delivering to Dumps, (Div'l Troops - Lihola Ble - Sei'bd Ble - Canadian Ble - to VILLERS BRETONNEUX - WARFUSÉE ABANCOURT - BAYONVILLERS and CAPPY respectively.) Provided 3 lorries to convey men from various Blos to CERISY for removals and 10 lorries to cut wood from BOIS GRESSAIRE. - Roads in bad condition near the wood - so returned empty to Parks. Inspected Buffalo traffic. Fine - great dust during night.	
"	2/7/7		Moved to MARCÉLCAVE in the afternoon - Canadian Section delivered.	
MARCELCAVE	3/7/7		"6" Section loaded. "B" Section delivered - Heavy fall of snow today. Inspected Canadian Section & Column.	
"	4/7/7		Nothing to report.	
"	5/7/7		"C" Section delivered and loaded - all "B" Section lorries engaged under French Army orders moving 8th Corps Ammo Dumps to ——. Weather fine	
TINCOURT				
"	6/7/7		Fine - "C" and "B" Section carried out work as yesterday. Also loaded & delivered to Ble Dumps 90 tons of Coal.	

T.1131. Wt. W708-776. 500000. 4/15. Sir J. C. & 9.

Army Form C. 2118.

5TH CAVALRY SUPPLY COLUMN.
No............
Date............

WAR DIARY
or
INTELLIGENCE SUMMARY.
(Erase heading not required.)

Instructions regarding War Diaries and Intelligence Summaries are contained in F.S. Regs., Part II. and the Staff Manual respectively. Title pages will be prepared in manuscript.

Place	Date	Hour	Summary of Events and Information	Remarks and references to Appendices
MARCELCAVE	6/7		Court martial sitting today on Pte DUFEY (Butcher Section) absented and A.Q.M. GIBBS and Pte STEVENS - awarded 168 yrs. imprisonment, public court. Baths outing from 10-30 am till 1-0 pm. Section Motor wheels by 3/2	
"	7/7		Church Parade of "A" "B" Sections - Men of Lieut HUNT and Lieut GIBSON sections attended at Butler - "B" Section Parades 9 horses & Mules to veterinary stores for casting ranks - 8 horses taken. Quirks and other horses & Cavalry Corps - 20 R.B.E. to transit camp 4 Div lost. B.A.C. (24th Div) "B" Section lost by the 17th 329 engineers (cancelled) in full. Column going to 17th & 349 engineers. Mules relieving 620 all ranks (19 extra wheels -6 attached).	
PROYART	8/7		Fine - Moved back to PROYART. "A" Section loaded at usual Railhead (LA FLAQUE) at 8 am. "B" Section 9/- loaded 38 lorries proceeded to VRAIGNES and COULAINCOURT nr VERMAND	

Army Form C. 2118.

5TH CAVALRY SUPPLY COLUMN.
No...........
Date.........

WAR DIARY
or
INTELLIGENCE SUMMARY.
(Erase heading not required.)

Instructions regarding War Diaries and Intelligence Summaries are contained in F.S. Regs. Part II. and the Staff Manual respectively. Title pages will be prepared in manuscript.

Place	Date	Hour	Summary of Events and Information	Remarks and references to Appendices
PROYART	8/7/		to pick up refugees luggage + bring it back to ...... Prichard at LA FLAQUE.	
"	9/7/		Showery. - provided 50 lorries for conveying NISSEN huts to III Corps to forward area.	
"	10/7/		Butels Section loaded at usual his place. - Warden's Section delivered to road dumps at 11 a.m. - provided 1 lorry for road-mending party to go to ESTREES-en-CHAUSEE.	
"	11/7/		Loaded & delivered as usual - "C" & "D" Sections respectively. Weather very wet-cold. Received instructions in evening to move by NESLE, which are cancelled later on. Enn / train.	
"	12/7/		Many enemy stragglers today. - "B" loaded at 9-20 am. and Prichard (LA FLAQUE) "C" Section delivered at 11 am.	
"	13/7/		Opened fine. "C" Section loaded at 9-20 a.m. They carried on workshops - due to the continual usage they are having.
			conveying NISSEN huts and extra forage, hospital fittings etc. A.D.S.S./Fortis/C.2118

Army Form C. 2118.

5TH CAVALRY SUPPLY COLUMN.

WAR DIARY
or
INTELLIGENCE SUMMARY.
(Erase heading not required.)

Place	Date	Hour	Summary of Events and Information	Remarks and references to Appendices
PROYART	13/7		"B" Section u/s to wound killed at 11 am.	
	14/7		Her horses returning hilts today. Division were known to your area. Fine. "B" Section delivered to new area nearest FRESNES-today. at 7 pm provided 1 lorry from "D" Type & gun to fire and one to A.D.M.S - "B" Section loaded as usual "B" Section lorries returned from delivery supplies about 10 pm - average mileage per lorry 70 miles	
HERLY 1 kilometre from NESLE	15/7		During all day - "B" Section loaded at NESLE w/am Column Headquarters & "B" Section moved to new bivouac by HERLY near NESLE, after delivering to new area. Tops. men living in dug-outs.	
	16/7		Wet - "B" Section delivered to usual area at usual time. "B" Section loaded at 10-30 am.	
	17/7		joined column from PROYART. "B" Section loaded at 9 am. "B" Section u/s at usual time.	

Army Form C. 2118.

5TH CAVALRY
SUPPLY COLUMN.
No..................
Date.................

WAR DIARY
or
INTELLIGENCE SUMMARY.
(Erase heading not required.)

Instructions regarding War Diaries and Intelligence Summaries are contained in F. S. Regs., Part II. and the Staff Manual respectively. Title pages will be prepared in manuscript.

Place	Date	Hour	Summary of Events and Information	Remarks and references to Appendices
HERLY	18/7/17		Met "B" Echelon loaded at NESLE at 5-30 a.m. "B" Echelon Section up to work to unload. Army to have several TENTS. Placed under charge of Sgt & hurried away to large supply line dumps nearby where they been high enemy aeroplanes in vicinity.	
	19/7/17		Fair day - Lovatt Pte TOMPKINS (driver) run over by 3y truck "Rifle" gun was seeking his spare horse showing weakness distress - enough by [III] troops military police to be not. "B" section trucks to mount line green.	
			"B" Echelon s/h no work.	
	20/7/17		Fine - usual routine	
	21/7/17		Fine - ditto	
	2.25		Fine - "B" Section	
			"B" Echelon ord to wound line (5 m) at NESLE Rations loaded moved plates except trucks Rec'd Rates, which were delivered to new dump 500 yds W.	
			of MONTECOURT. 2 lorries returned from duty	

2353 Wt. W2544/1454 700,000 5/15 D. D. & L.   A.D.S.S./Forms/C. 2118.

WAR DIARY or INTELLIGENCE SUMMARY

Army Form C. 2118.

5TH CAVALRY SUPPLY COLUMN.

Place	Date	Hour	Summary of Events and Information	Remarks and references to Appendices
HERLY	23/7/17		2nd L. of C. at FEUQUIERES (in back area)	
	23/7/17		Received broken lorry in replacement of COMBER lorry evacuated several days ago.	
	24/7/17		Received authority to evacuate 4 G.O.G. lorry No 9747 "B" Section loaded as usual — "B" Section d/d to motor dumps. Capt H.G. STAFFORD (i/c Bodies Section) reported from Hospital.	
			1st — exchanged keen lorry for new Commer lorry with the Army Pack line just received. "B" Section loaded & "B" Section delivered at usual times w/where. Received intimation from Gardens A.D.M.S. that Capt H.P. BLACKWOOD. A.S.C. had been admitted to Hospital also suffering from V.D.S.	
	25/7/17		Dull & cooler — Loading & delivery as usual — After "B" Section had ⅞ loaded, air lines loaded 11½ tons Iron Rations & other articles and delivered to dumps at TREFCON	

Army Form C. 2118.

5TH CAVALRY SUPPLY COLUMN.

WAR DIARY
or
INTELLIGENCE SUMMARY.
(Erase heading not required.)

Place	Date	Hour	Summary of Events and Information	Remarks and references to Appendices
HEALY	26/7		Fine — Loading & delivery as usual. "b" Section, after delivering, picked up another 14 tons from Crow ration & gun and delivered them to TREFCON. Lieut Ballender - Young (Canadian Section 5th Div. Supply Col) proceeded to join the 2nd Canadian Div: Supply Column.	
	27/7		Dull but fine — "b" Section loaded at 6 am — "B" Section delivered as usual.	
	28/7		Fine — loading & delivering as usual. {Lt AA. GREGORY reported sick Hospital & Lt R.C. KEEFE proceeded from Flight Depot	
	29/7		Fine: "B" Section delivered as usual. "b" Section ladded at 6 am and delivered some say at 2 pm to send dumps. One section of column will, until further orders, load & deliver the same day. Lieut L.G. DEACON (C.A.S.C) reported for duty.	
	30/7		Fine: "B" Section loaded at 6 am & delivered to usual dumps. The spare section ("b") provided 30 lorries, which were placed at the 7 disposal of S.M.T.O. II Corps for various duties — chiefly R.E. They also provided	

Army Form C. 2118.

WAR DIARY
or
INTELLIGENCE SUMMARY.
(Erase heading not required.)

5TH CAVALRY
SUPPLY COLUMN.
No............
Date...........

Instructions regarding War Diaries and Intelligence Summaries are contained in F. S. Regs., Part II. and the Staff Manual respectively. Title pages will be prepared in manuscript.

Place	Date	Hour	Summary of Events and Information	Remarks and references to Appendices
HÉRLY	30/4		provided 1 additional horses for today relieving by return from Rialland Cavgh Tuint (all ranks) 616.	

V McArthur
MAJOR.
O.C. 5th CAV. SUPPLY COL.

5th Div Train Sup [Col?]

Army Form C. 2118.

WAR DIARY
or
INTELLIGENCE SUMMARY.

Vol. XI

(Erase heading not required.)

Place	Date	Hour	Summary of Events and Information	Remarks and references to Appendices
HERLY (SOMME)	1/7		Weather still continues fine. "B" Section loaded at 6am and delivered to usual billets at 3 pm. I was trying to get the latter time altered to 12 noon or earlier, in order that the horses may proceed direct from the billets to the various lorries. "C" Section provided 20 horses for various duties under instructions from S.M.T.O. IV Corps.	
	2/7		Lecture by Gas Officer. "B" Section loaded at 4-30 am & delivered to yesterday. "B" Section provided 20 horses for similar duties to those required yesterday.	
			Weather fine –	
	3/7		Fine – duties as yesterday –	
	4/7		explosion of a bomb which some men of the barnham Section were tampering with, contrary to existing orders. – Pte Breeze injured by	
	5/7		Fine – Routine as usual.	
	6/7		Fine – " " "	

Army Form C. 2118.

WAR DIARY
or
INTELLIGENCE SUMMARY.
(Erase heading not required.)

Place	Date	Hour	Summary of Events and Information	Remarks and references to Appendices
HERLY	7/8/17		Fine - Section changed over duties - begin'n Britt's section	
		11-30 am	& delivering to group dumps at 11 am. Britt's section provided 30 lorries for R.E. duties under instructions from S.M.T.O. DI Corps. Also 16 lorries to move documents reinforcements	
	9/5/17		from dumps near BRIE to BOIS D'HOLNON - to Kilometre from the line. It further 4 lorries (2 from each section) to deliver Oats water straw to the Dumps.	
	10/5/17		Wet - Routine as usual. Lt. J. Oliver admitted to hospital as result of accident to knee.	
	11/5/17		Wet - Routine as usual.	
			Fine - Provided 22 lorries only for S.M.T.O. & for heavy bde. from CAIX to this area.	
	12/5/17		Fine - Routine as usual. Only provided 6 lorries for S.M.T.O.	
MONCHAIN	13/5/17		Fine - "B" section baled delivered as usual - provided 14 lorries	
MONCHAIN	13/5/17		For date from CAIX & 6 lorries from S.M.T.O. IV Corps. Moved to new billets at MONCHAIN (about 6 Kilos N.E. of NESLE) under orders of the	

WAR DIARY
or
INTELLIGENCE SUMMARY

Army Form C. 2118.

Place	Date	Hour	Summary of Events and Information	Remarks and references to Appendices
MONCHAIN	13/3/17		To O.C. H.Q. — the village has been totally destroyed by bombardment etc., the unit is totally under canvas. Two very large craters in the village make transport difficult.	
Nr NESLE	14/3/17		Stormy afternoon. An "extraordinarily severe storm accompanied by most vivid lightning and tropical rain broke over the country about 3-30 am. & lasted for an hour. Two marquees & one of two tents were blown down. The occupants escaped injury. "C" Section provided 18 lorries & "B" Section loaded & delivered several old lorries. "B" Section provided 7 lorries for the L.M.T.O. 51 Corps & as usual. Routine as usual.	
	15/3/17		Went to Montenescourt. Major Gunn REGNIER-ECLUSE (5 miles N.W. of CRECY) Abbeville area - to VILLERS BRETTONNEUX. Made a complaint to O.C. Field Y. ambulance to proper authorities regarding the treatment meted out to the drivers & 13 lorries which provided to DUISANS near ARRAS to meet new lorry convoys. The new lorries were working from 10 am on 12th inst. (line of having HERLY) till 3-30 pm	

WAR DIARY
or
INTELLIGENCE SUMMARY.
(Erase heading not required.)

Army Form C. 2118.

Place	Date	Hour	Summary of Events and Information	Remarks and references to Appendices
MONCHAIN	15/7		On 14th inst (41½ hours) work but 3 hours intermission granted to all in line whenever attached to this unit. Dumped supplies in DEVISE-MERAUCOURT road as under:	
			AMBALA Bde (rear group) at 11-30 a.m.	
			SEC. BAD " "	
			CANADIAN " "	
			DIVL TROOPS " "	
		at 11-30 am	a/d supplies at Divl Rec dump at TREFCON & SEC. BAD Bde (forward group) "	
			CANADIAN " "	
			Lt. R.C. KEEFE on command to Divl A.S.C. Hqrs.	
			Lt. G.E. NESBITT rejoined Divl A.S.C. Hqrs yesterday.	
			Proceeded Lorry to YMCA NESLE. Applied for issue of Lime juice stores weekly.	
	16/7		Routine as yesterday re loading & delivering supplies (B Lot)	
			"C" Lot provided 16 lorries for various duties.	
			A.D.S.S. outlined issue of Lime juice twice weekly.	

Army Form C. 2118.

WAR DIARY
or
INTELLIGENCE SUMMARY.
(Erase heading not required.)

Instructions regarding War Diaries and Intelligence Summaries are contained in F. S. Regs., Part II. and the Staff Manual respectively. Title pages will be prepared in manuscript.

Place	Date	Hour	Summary of Events and Information	Remarks and references to Appendices
MONCHAIN	17/5/17		Heavy hail. Cooler. A.D.M.S. continued home & run to Div. H.Q. "B" Sec. loaded (NESLE 4-30 am) & delivered supplies at 11-30 as yesterday. "B" Sec. provided 30 odd lorries for extraneous duties. Orders received from 14 Kb to provide the troops falling forward tender with 1000 empty petrol tins for water. There is no in addition to 2000 supplied yesterday.	
	18/5/17		Fine. "B" Sec. held delivered as usual — also in addition 2 batteries started from 4th Inn. Div. "C" Section engaged in extraneous duties as usual.	
	19/5/17		Fine. "B" Sec. loads delivered as usual. "C" Section in extraneous duties. Motor van arrangements made by the A.D.S.T. Workshops. All application for extraneous duties, must from the 19th inst., be made to him by 9 am previous to the day required. If lists & available lorries is sent to the A.D.S.T. by us before 2 pm daily, & a roster of duties, based upon these, is sent in the evening for the duty tomorrow.	

WAR DIARY or INTELLIGENCE SUMMARY

Army Form C. 2118.

(Erase heading not required.)

Place	Date	Hour	Summary of Events and Information	Remarks and references to Appendices
MONCHAIN	20/5/17		Fine - hot. "B" Sect. loaded at 6-30 am NESLE & delivered to usual groups dumps. IV Corps mounted troops reserved heavy batteries attached to the Div. 7 lorries reported for testing purposes today. "B" Sect. provided only 6 lorries for reconnaissance duties for low temp - + 1 (under orders of the O.C. A.B.) got moving Liaison Officers hit to Div. Hqrs supplying Lt. Col. attached to "B" Section & moving like to the non Hqrs engaged & attached radio and D.T. details.	
	21/5/17		Fine - Routine as usual.	
	22/5/17		Well - "B" Section loaded at NESLE & delivered to usual hills. "B" Section sent additional lorries to "B" Section to assist with the increased loading capacity due to attachment of 4th Div. Div. Q & U Batteries + I.A.A. Column. Column moved to new hills to MONCHY-LAGACHE	
MONCHY LAGACHE	23/5/17		Fine - "B" loaded at ROISEL at 8.45 am + delivered to usual dumps. "B" Section provided 20 lorries for extraneous duties	

Army Form C. 2118.

WAR DIARY
or
INTELLIGENCE SUMMARY.
(Erase heading not required.)

Instructions regarding War Diaries and Intelligence Summaries are contained in F.S. Regs., Part II. and the Staff Manual respectively. Title pages will be prepared in manuscript.

Place	Date	Hour	Summary of Events and Information	Remarks and references to Appendices
MONCHY-LAGACHE	23/5/17		Workshops quartered comfortably in all larger factory — lecture under canvas. Villages in ruins here — secured the only place with a roof on in the neighbourhood.	
"	24/5/17		Fine — "B" lecture under returned to work — S.	
"	25/5/17		Fine — Lieut. ⟨?⟩ PELLETTE — Routine — "B" engaged on various interior duties.	
"	26/5/17		Fine — ordered all ranks to wear Box Respirators in the "alert" position for 10 min. Fox Rs "P" & "P" at 10 am.	
"			Routine as usual — got this "P" at 10 am. ⟨?⟩ another 300 empty Petrol tins (in addition to 400 not yet salvaged) to Forward dumps, to save us a return respirator in the trenches. (Bundance + Lee ⟨?⟩ left Petrol.)	
"	27/5/17		Fine — Routine as usual — 1st "Y" type Gas mask would you employ from D.S.C. for packing their details in the case. 23 boxes employing II boxes tunicles. Trimeon with this weeding to be repaired to XIV B.T.S.C.	
"	28/5/17		Fine — no work — no enemy — routine as usual "B" + "C" lecture returned to duties.	

WAR DIARY
or
INTELLIGENCE SUMMARY
(Erase heading not required.)

Army Form C. 2118.

Place	Date	Hour	Summary of Events and Information	Remarks and references to Appendices
MONCHY-LAGACHE	29/7		Fine - cool. British letters landing at LA CHAPELLETTE at 9 am and delivering at 11 am to usual dumps. Tandem to various retaining statios from the Goodergee.	
"	30/7		Fog. Rations as usual except that into the Res troop today, ad in patres, from Fuls Supply Dept FROISSY-PELTER issued with "P.H. Helmets" thing - these in addition to Resp. Repiratus.	
"	31/7		Fine - Loading. Delivering as usual. The following units are to draw today - 63rd H.A. Group, 115th H.B., 249th H.A. group, 1/1st London H.A., 110th H.A. Btty, 91b Siege Btty, 114th Siege Btty, 119th Siege Btty. All Blue Cord strengths of units = 612 all ranks. All Blue Cord Passes returned to A.P.M. 5th Cavn Divn.	

J. Marshall
MAJOR.
O.C. 5th CAV. SUPPLY COL.

5TH CAVALRY
SUPPLY COLUMN.

Army Form C. 2118.

WAR DIARY
or
INTELLIGENCE SUMMARY.
(Erase heading not required.)

Instructions regarding War Diaries and Intelligence Summaries are contained in F.S. Regs., Part II. and the Staff Manual respectively. Title pages will be prepared in manuscript.

Place	Date	Hour	Summary of Events and Information	Remarks and references to Appendices
MONCHY- LAGACHE	1/6/17		Fine – "British" Section loading (at LA CHAPELETTE) & delivering supplies. "Indians" Sec: engaged on strenuous duties.	
"	2/6/17		Yesterday's tempo	
"	3/6/17		Fine – do quietly. String of tent-attendants – 610.	
"	4/6/17		2nd – do usual.	
"	5/6/17		Fine – reply to enquiries & recd.	
"	6/6/17		Sections exchanged duties –	
"			"B" Section re supplies. "A" Section re ATHIES CH. (O'c woke two) appointed Cap (ie Sec) –	
"			Section on strenuous duties – Military the large drafts (Men Sec) so reported on diff.	
"	6/6/17		Stormy – usual routine.	
"	7/6/17		Fine – hot – "	
"	8/6/17		Fine – hot – "	
"	9/6/17		Fine – hot – " = strength of unit 609 all ranks.	
"			The "Column towards Paty (Fr Sous Peltima) & Brestia gave a successful show this evening before an audience of between 500–700 men.	
"	10/6/17		Fine – Morning of importance to record.	
"	11/6/17		Stormy – "	

Army Form C. 2118.

WAR DIARY
or
INTELLIGENCE SUMMARY.
(Erase heading not required.)

Instructions regarding War Diaries and Intelligence Summaries are contained in F. S. Regs., Part II. and the Staff Manual respectively. Title pages will be prepared in manuscript.

Place	Date	Hour	Summary of Events and Information	Remarks and references to Appendices
MONCHY-LAGACHE	12/7/17		Fine - bellions exchanged duties - "B" bet. today delivering supplies to "C" bet. the extraneous duties on R.E. etc.	
" "	13/7/17		Fine - usual routine.	
" "	14/7/17		Fine - " "	
" "	15/7/17		Fine - " "	
" "	16/7/17		Fine - very hot - usual routine - Strength (all ranks) = 603	
" "	17/7/17		Fine - " "	
" "	18/7/17		Fine - " "	
" "	19/7/17		Stormy - sections exchanged duties - "B" bet. today relieving the bet. extraneous duties. Major V.M. HUTTON. D.S.O. proceeded on leave.	
" "	20/7/17		Fine - cooler - Pte. Roberton granted 5 days extension of leave.	
" "	21/7/17		Wet - usual routine	
" "	22/7/17		Fine - " "	
" "	23/7/17		" - "	

Army Form C. 2118.

WAR DIARY
or
INTELLIGENCE SUMMARY.
(Erase heading not required.)

Instructions regarding War Diaries and Intelligence Summaries are contained in F. S. Regs., Part II. and the Staff Manual respectively. Title pages will be prepared in manuscript.

Place	Date	Hour	Summary of Events and Information	Remarks and references to Appendices
MONCHY-LAGACHE	25/6/17		Weather fine. Advised that the Battalion is to attend a Medical Board in England to have its invalidity recorded.	
" "	26/6/17		Weather fine. Shelters on through better - Loading & detraining supplies tramcars Station performing the usual routine duties.	
" "	26/6/17		Weather fine - hot cooler - usual routine.	
" "	27/6/17		" " - strength returns but all ranks - usual routine.	
" "	27/6/17		Weather fine - thunderstorm broke over later - submitted returns of leave - 11 other ranks proceeded home during June - 13 men on roll have not had leave for over 18 months, while 30 (inclusive of the 13) have not had leave for 12 months, and 62 12 months. The leave question is a very difficult one, especially as much application on long received for leave on urgent private affairs this the are very small allotment of vacancies.	

Army Form C. 2118.

WAR DIARY
or
INTELLIGENCE SUMMARY.
(Erase heading not required.)

Place	Date	Hour	Summary of Events and Information	Remarks and references to Appendices
MONCHY - LAGACHE	28th/7		Quiet on the west. Lieut. Y. G. Robertson having attended Medical Board in England is struck off strength with effect from 19-4-17 under provisions of G.R.O. 23 ad 2nd - ward notice.	
- " -	29th/7		Not very well. —	
- " -	30th/7		Received wire addressed Capt THIEPSCH & your all. Received wire addressed "Capt July — no improvement on June. I am anxious on your a/c I consider risks (including 2 in the letter of 14 yesterday unless expired men 2 "2" opened" leave vacancies you urgent private affairs) — not total is break up squad 400 men as these let me know you are 12 weeks supply 2 yours = 2.! Column to be inspected by G.O.C on 31st prox.	W. Mapford Lieut O.C. 5th CAV. SUPPLY COL.

5TH CAVALRY SUPPLY COLUMN.

WAR DIARY
or
INTELLIGENCE SUMMARY.

(Erase heading not required.)

Army Form C. 2118.

Instructions regarding War Diaries and Intelligence Summaries are contained in F.S. Regs., Part II. and the Staff Manual respectively. Title pages will be prepared in manuscript.

Place	Date	Hour	Summary of Events and Information	Remarks and references to Appendices
MONCHY-LAGACHE	1/2/17		Fine – routine as usual.	
	2/2/17		Unyield –	
	3/2/17		Fine – section exchanged duties ("B" section on entraining duties "C" section training delivering supplies)	
	3/2/17		Fine: Major HUTTON reported from leave	
	4/17		Fine: Column inspected at 3-30 pm by Brig-Gen. H.J.M. McLellan ISO	
	5/2/17		¼ sunday O.C.	
			Fine – Usual routine.	
	6/2/17		Fine – strong – 2/Lt. CLAUDE LEVY joined unit from M.T. School of Instruction	
	7/17		Fine – Lieut. D. SHEPHERD Canadian A.S.C. joined unit from London temps deps column inspected ? to bowden ?	
			Lieut R.C. KEEFE RSC struck off strength with effect from today + transferred to field headqrs. S.P. Comdr.	
	8/2/17		Wet – very stormy –	
	9/2/17		Fine – nothing to report.	

Army Form C. 2118.

WAR DIARY
or
INTELLIGENCE SUMMARY.
(Erase heading not required.)

Instructions regarding War Diaries and Intelligence Summaries are contained in F. S. Regs., Part II. and the Staff Manual respectively. Title pages will be prepared in manuscript.

Place	Date	Hour	Summary of Events and Information	Remarks and references to Appendices
MONCHY- LAGACHE	10/7		Fair – received revised establishment – which reduces to establishment by 2 transport officers – 2 batmen – 8 M.T. drivers – only 1 driver for workshops & store lorry men being attached instead. P. 3 as previously.	
	11/7		Fine – nothing to report.	
	12/7		Fine – entrances duty forenoon. Loading and behaviour in double echelon from lorry onwards.	
	13/7		Stormy – as yesterday.	
	14/7		Fine – Division move to new area around ST. POL. today.	
			"B" Ech'n 4/1 and camped at PROYART.	
	15/7		Fine – "D" Ech'n 4/1 & camped at LEALVILLERS.	
ST. POL	16/7		Fine – Headquarters eschelons moved to ST POL. and present	
			by "C" Eschelon.	
	17/7		Dull – "B" Eschelon joined rest of column after delivering	
	18/7		" – new order, usual routine.	
	19/7		Fine – held inspection of "C" Eschelon to identify a man after case	

WAR DIARY
or
INTELLIGENCE SUMMARY.

(Erase heading not required.)

Army Form C. 2118.

Place	Date	Hour	Summary of Events and Information	Remarks and references to Appendices
ST. POL	19/7		Rode which received in Sept last night. One man admitted by French civilian and an officer. J. Lumsey & another also straying. M. J.M. unimportant.	
	20/7		Fine – round units. Received orders from 1/S Dr. by M. Kelly horses to sent over Jumelles here are a great shortage of tufts orgs they report.	
	21/7		Fine – round units being increased to 53rd Lgt of the Div'n. Strength returns 598 all ranks. 387 men out of 523 (exc. of stretcher) apts & how the unit is many over.	
			I leave one the unit to UK for 4 weeks & over, whilst 27 T have more have not let leave yet 18 month's leave. Our total allotments by mumbers of July is only 20 to date.	
	22/7 23/7 24/7		Fine – raining & importance to report. Indt – usual routine. Duel call – "B" Section attached on transvere duties near ALBERT – "A" Section Loading & MG on single echelon.	

Army Form C. 2118.

WAR DIARY
or
INTELLIGENCE SUMMARY.
(Erase heading not required.)

Instructions regarding War Diaries and Intelligence Summaries are contained in F. S. Regs., Part II. and the Staff Manual respectively. Title pages will be prepared in manuscript.

Place	Date	Hour	Summary of Events and Information	Remarks and references to Appendices
ST. POL	25/7		Fine — usual routine	
	26/7		Fine — " "	
	27/7		Fine — "B" Echelon reported balloon — lorry & delivering an alternate hoop net to "B" Echelon	
	28/7		Fair — usual routine — sent 2 men of Lorries Length to units 598 all ranks. Reqd to have to work to Lieut of Lt. Duncan (Canadian Section of the unit) on hospital at FREVENT early this morning. Your Servants	
	29/7		Fair — nothing of importance to record. Funeral of 96 Duncan this afternoon — all officers attended	
	30/7		Wet — usual routine	
	31/7		Fine — HQrs of Our moved to HEUCHIN — proceeded & Lorries to visit thereon etc., Strength Establ. = 598 all ranks	

VMWhite
MAJOR
O.C. 5th CAV. SUPPLY COL.

2353 Wt. W3544/1454 700,000 5/15 D.D.&L. A.D.S.S./Forms/C. 2118.

War Diary / Intelligence Summary

Army Form C. 2118.

5TH CAVALRY SUPPLY COLUMN

Instructions regarding War Diaries and Intelligence Summaries are contained in F.S. Regs., Part II. and the Staff Manual respectively. Title pages will be prepared in manuscript.

Place	Date	Hour	Summary of Events and Information	Remarks and references to Appendices
ST. POL	1/8/17		Still very wet — usual routine. — 2Lt Shepherd assumed command of "B" Ect.	"B" Ect.
	2/8/17		" "	
	3/8/17		City wet — much cooler — 6 men (18 months with without any leave) proceed on 10 days leave to U.K. today at 13.10 am	
	4/8/17		Wet & cold — another 8 men proceeded on leave — routine as usual. — Strength of unit (all ranks) 596.	
	5/8/17		Fair — weather improving — usual routine	
	6/8/17		Fair — sending 32 men on leave to U.K. today as tomorrow — men will have collected and work letter the returned leave parties. No interpreter found will be attached as well from being so inaccurate to	
	7/8/17		Fine — too hot Lieut Gregory (as Supply Officer).	
	8/8/17		Fine — usual routine.	
	9/8/17		Showery — usual routine.	
	10/8/17		Wet — raining & impossible to unload.	
	11/8/17		Fine — Strength of Column 596 all ranks — am expected to be	

2353 Wt. W2544/1454 700,000 5/15 D. D. & L. A.D.S.S./Forms/C. 2118.

WAR DIARY or INTELLIGENCE SUMMARY

Army Form C. 2118.

5TH CAVALRY SUPPLY COLUMN.

Place	Date	Hour	Summary of Events and Information	Remarks and references to Appendices
ST. POL.	11/7 (cont)		A.A.G. Havelian Section here that no further requirements will be sent up until the Section Est^t establishment has been achieved.	
	12/7		Fine – today is noted.	
	13/7		Fine – received orders 10 lorries convoys for 19³ inst. will note 21 men equipped line the unit reports to 14³ inst.	
	14/7		Fine – routine no news. Kelly leaving ("C" Section) going on 1st Siege Gⁿ lorries – to be shown to Dio Horse then tomorrow	
	15/7		Dull – showery – Divisional Horse Shoe an BRYAS – proceeded 30 pcs. lorries conveying troops & supports then 28mm on each Duty Orderlies but to the Show.	
	16/7		Dull – all usual routine.	
	17/7		" "	
			Fine – 17³ 18³ 19³ inst. – sending 465 men went on leave	
	18/7		Fine – usual routine.	

Army Form C. 2118.

WAR DIARY
or
INTELLIGENCE SUMMARY.
(Erase heading not required.)

Instructions regarding War Diaries and Intelligence Summaries are contained in F. S. Regs., Part II. and the Staff Manual respectively. Title pages will be prepared in manuscript.

Place	Date	Hour	Summary of Events and Information	Remarks and references to Appendices
ST. POL.	19/7		Fine - strength went 590 all ranks. Lorham arrived.	
	20/7		Fine - today - pieces 84 very successfully. "Bonner" lorry No. 38499 succeeded to run in due to damage	
	21/7		Fine - entered on a collision and Lieu. Supplement pushed tie. usual routine. 7th C. LEM departed to join	
	22/7		No. 34 Q received supply lorries.	
	23/7		Fine - Rec - usual routine.	
			Fine - Received instruction to send 5th lorries - there to move to Aire August have departed 8th - reinforcement as specially marked.	
	24/7		Fine - usual routine	
	25/7		"	
	26/7		"	
	27/7		hot - big storm nature arrived	
	28/7		Wet - usual routine - lorry stopped	
	29/7		Fine - sent 13 out to Rear M.T Depot in accordance with No. 4.T. instructions (see diary)	

2353. Wt. W2544/1454 700,000 5/15 D. D. & L. A.D.S.S./Forms/C.2118.

Army Form C. 2118.

WAR DIARY
or
INTELLIGENCE SUMMARY.
(Erase heading not required.)

Instructions regarding War Diaries and Intelligence Summaries are contained in F. S. Regs., Part II. and the Staff Manual respectively. Title pages will be prepared in manuscript.

5TH CAVALRY
SUPPLY COLUMN

No...........
Date.........

Place	Date	Hour	Summary of Events and Information	Remarks and references to Appendices
ST. POL	30/9/17		Wet - usual routine - leur re-joined line and 19/4 NCOs went on leave during the month - no rider 31 men also had been selected - leave for 18 months. Dull - one ran remaining 13 men to Base M.T. Depot. Strength to follow. (all ranks) = 562 - 142 lorries - 4 lines, 2 motor cycles - 1 M/c sidecar.	

[signature]
O.C. 5TH CAV. SUPPLY COL.
MAJOR

WAR DIARY or INTELLIGENCE SUMMARY

(Erase heading not required.)

Army Form C. 2118.

Serial No. 56.

5TH CAVALRY SUPPLY COLUMN.

Place	Date	Hour	Summary of Events and Information	Remarks and references to Appendices
ST. POL	1/7		Fine - usual routine. Paraded 50 o.r. horses for Divisional 3 troops to Y Gun Lumping Corps. Horse shoe full etc.	
	2/7		RAME COURT. Fine - sent 10 men or horse tonight.	
	3/7		Fine - usual routine. Sent another 10 men or horses tonight.	
			- Also leaves 105 men on to visit 12 horse him in France over 12 months without leave.	
	4/7		Fuller - Leave via Boulogne extended - leave party held back.	
	5/7		Fine - usual routine - leave re-opened.	
			Fine - stormy later - received notification than no S.O.S., Lumping Corps, than to supply personnel etc, at present number 150 2 the establishment, we to be reduced by 20.	
	6/7		Stormy - not - usual routine	
	7/7		Dull - usual routine	
	8/7		Fine " " - strength of unit = 556 all ranks	
	9/7		Fine " "	

WAR DIARY
or
INTELLIGENCE SUMMARY
(Erase heading not required.)

Army Form C. 2118.

5TH CAVALRY SUPPLY COLUMN

Place	Date	Hour	Summary of Events and Information	Remarks and references to Appendices
ST. POL.	10/7		Fine – Reveived satisfactory charge. Supply col. established rails. he reserved by 1 Gnr and 2 Indian cyclists as temporary measure.	
	11/7		Fine – Normal routine – reserved with 21 Indian recruits. Sat 14½ to 18½ inds.	
	12/7		Fine – usual routine.	
	13/7		Dull – " "	
	14/"		" "	
	15/"		Fine – a fire occurred to a short stack about 100 yards from our lines. Extinguished with aid of 2 Pyres and orderlies. Small portion of stack. Was believed to have been caused by some French children who were playing around. Reported immediately to the Division.	
	16/7		Dull – Received an usual strength Column. 350 all ranks evacuated to base 14 Pyrels [cavalry] as reinfts to the return in establishment of the Column.	

5TH CAVALRY
SUPPLY COLUMN.
Army Form C. 2118.

WAR DIARY
or
INTELLIGENCE SUMMARY.
(Erase heading not required.)

Instructions regarding War Diaries and Intelligence Summaries are contained in F.S. Regs., Part II. and the Staff Manual respectively. Title pages will be prepared in manuscript.

Place	Date	Hour	Summary of Events and Information	Remarks and references to Appendices
ST POL	17/7		Fine - usual routine	
	18/7		Fine - evacuated hill to Bridgeville on Bullers command. moved to Bridgeville on ST POL - PREVENT Road (a hutted billet Chasse the plans 4 + 3 Brig. Shan to rest for the lordinmen)	
	19/7		Fine - usual routine - returned billets in Lov. est BHQ. 2 personnel	
	20/7		Fine - cooler - " "	
	21/7		Fine " " Capt Chipter reported to take command of lorry section - relief Lieut Legrand - at present on leave, also on to be repat to to London lorries T.S.C. has return.	
	22/7		Fine - usual routine - strength to Column 13 officers 534 o.r. - does not include M.O. also on storek by to strength	
	23/7		Sent 22 men on leave (all 15 workingmen)	
	24/7		Fine - usual routine	
	25/7		Fine - " "	
	26/7		Dine - " "	

Army Form C. 2118.

[Stamp: 5TH CAVALRY SUPPLY COLUMN.]

WAR DIARY
or
INTELLIGENCE SUMMARY.
(Erase heading not required.)

Instructions regarding War Diaries and Intelligence Summaries are contained in F. S. Regs., Part II. and the Staff Manual respectively. Title pages will be prepared in manuscript.

Place	Date	Hour	Summary of Events and Information	Remarks and references to Appendices
ST. POL.	27/7/17		Fine – Major Poulton as Major to base – examined by M.O. upon return from leave on 14th October.	
	28/7/17		Received instructions from A.D.S.T. to send the F.O. empties tomorrow to S.M.T.D. X Corps – Weather continue.	
	29/7/17		Fine – Received lorries to collect and deliver rounds the Division.	
	30/7/17		16 bns of Oiva Issued from NIEPPE sur CAICHE – 9 O.R.'s proceeded on leave. 8 O.R.'s proceeded on leave. Lorry car 17315 evacuated to A.D. of T. workshops. Feb car 27315 Ford sent to Signal Squadron to replace	

[Signature]
MAJOR
O.C. 5th CAV. SUPPLY COL.

A.D.S.S./Forms/C. 2118.

Army Form C. 2118.

WAR DIARY
or
INTELLIGENCE SUMMARY.

5th Cavalry Division Supply Column

October 1917

(Erase heading not required.)

Instructions regarding War Diaries and Intelligence Summaries are contained in F. S. Regs., Part II. and the Staff Manual respectively. Title pages will be prepared in manuscript.

Place	Date	Hour	Summary of Events and Information	Remarks and references to Appendices
ST POL	1/10/17		Fine — usual routine — 5 lorries proceeded to 4th Cav. Field Squadron for duty under C.R.E. Can. Corps.	
"	2/10/17		Fine — Jan 30 out lorries assisted daily to that had from the Central Ouahai Head — Jaw barracks left batmen for R.3 & A Hdqrs on probation.	
"	3/10/17		At Shepherd Canadian Section left unit to proceed and report for duty to Canadian Corps Supply Column.	
"	4/10/17		Fine — usual routine — Standing arm certificate from six Shepherd to Capt Chaplin forwarded to 2.i.c.a.s.c. at R.B.V. lodge temp attached to this unit proceeded on leave to U.K.	
"	5/10/17		Commenced loading on Monday reboteon — Capt Chaplin proceeded on leave to U.K. — 3 three ton lorries temp detached with field squadron — 'E' section of 'B' loading at St Pol proceeded to STEENBECQUE to detrain and park.	
	6/10/17		'B' Section left St Pol area after loading and proceeded to camp in STEENBECQUE area. — So so much heavy rain all day	

Army Form C. 2118.

WAR DIARY
or
INTELLIGENCE SUMMARY.
(Erase heading not required.)

Instructions regarding War Diaries and Intelligence Summaries are contained in F. S. Regs., Part II. and the Staff Manual respectively. Title pages will be prepared in manuscript.

Place	Date	Hour	Summary of Events and Information	Remarks and references to Appendices
St Pol	7/7/14		Winter time came into operation with effect from 1.0 a.m which became midnight 8/7. Hdqrs Column and Workshops moved from St Pol to WATOU. One in billets in WATOU. One in morning... very wet in the afternoon.	
WATOU	8/7/14		One in morning. All in in the afternoon. B section less Ambula Pole lorries moved into WATOU from STEENBECQUE - A lorries detached with field Squadron rejoined Column.	
"	9/7/14		Railhead for supplies WIPPENHOEK. Received instructions for supply officer and details to be billeted at W'hoek.	
"	10/7/14		One - normal routine	
"	11/7/14		"	
"	12/7/14		"	
"	13/7/14		"	
"	14/7/14		"	
"	15/7/14		Fine - Ambule supplies had Oil from supplies apt to reload a new ESSINGHEM. Division in the near future - further H turner to make it Oil W'hoek Oil...	

2353 Wt. W2544/1454 700,000 5/15 D. D. & L. A.D.S.S. Forms/C. 2118.

Army Form C. 2118.

WAR DIARY
or
INTELLIGENCE SUMMARY.
(Erase heading not required.)

Instructions regarding War Diaries and Intelligence Summaries are contained in F. S. Regs., Part II. and the Staff Manual respectively. Title pages will be prepared in manuscript.

Place	Date	Hour	Summary of Events and Information	Remarks and references to Appendices
WATOU (Belgium)	15/10/17	a.m.	Loaded at WIPERDHOEK — left for march to HESDIN. Arrived HESDIN.	
LUMBRES	16/10/17	a.m.	Left HESDIN — arrived at LUMBRES. Moved on after retaining proceed to LA LOGE — 5 kilos N. of HESDIN.	
LA LOGE	17/10/17	p.m.	HESDIN — All A Hosp billets AMBRINES VAST (Fr Vet.)	
"	18/10/17	a.m.	BOUT DE LA RUE (Horses) FRESSIN (ATS) FRUGES (St Bell) Hardelot Villacoublay as orderly boy — proceed to learn to cut harness types — 9 am. (9 hrs.) and 10 hrs. to dismantle, reassemble in BRILLEUL horses will proceed by return tr. 10 ½ a.m. Returned Dec. record P.H. Blendel — TADOS (460)	
"	19/10/17		"	
"	20/10/17		"	
"	21/10/17		"	

Army Form C. 2118.

WAR DIARY
or
INTELLIGENCE SUMMARY.
(Erase heading not required.)

Instructions regarding War Diaries and Intelligence Summaries are contained in F. S. Regs., Part II. and the Staff Manual respectively. Title pages will be prepared in manuscript.

Place	Date	Hour	Summary of Events and Information	Remarks and references to Appendices
LA LOGE	22/7/17	Fine	Went route - Major V.M. HUTTON, DSO. formerly Brant proceed to I.R. - Lt. G.W. CHAPLIN remaining doing duty.	
"	23/7/17	Dull	Today transport rested.	
"	24/7/17	dull	"	
"	25/7/17	Fine	Proved new lorries to bring horses hats to HESDIN. Received	
"	26/7/17	dull	'B' Echelon lorries delivered supplies in Divisional Schemel. Required instruction to horses wanted forthwith new stables for 52 Divl. Amm. Park. Bath. Pnltr. landed troops.) near YPRES.	
"	27/7/17	wet	On action hulled delivers	
"	28/7/17	Fine	Today Kitchen trench telegraph delivered Reserve was etting close to lines of telegraph.	
"	29/7/17	Dull	to regiment but on place bedded down	
"	30/7/17	wet	later delivered ordinary load was recipient had	
"			were sub train reveal ammunition. 2 horses passed from 2nd Army base turn supply column to replying at detachment Depot Horses lepulse Batt."	

Army Form C. 2118.

WAR DIARY
or
INTELLIGENCE SUMMARY.
(Erase heading not required.)

Instructions regarding War Diaries and Intelligence Summaries are contained in F. S. Regs., Part II and the Staff Manual respectively. Title pages will be prepared in manuscript.

Place	Date	Hour	Summary of Events and Information	Remarks and references to Appendices
LA LOGE	31/7/16		Usual routine. Strength 5+6 all ranks men and horses all well having the 1/2 months men. — a new experience, awaiting further instructions but much appreciated. No 9 L.A.C.B. Rebels attached to 5th Division stuck by strength and upper them 24-10-16 — proceeded to Opps Troops.	

V. Maxwell
Lt. Col.
S.S. 2nd CAV. SUPPLY COLN

Army Form C. 2118.

56

WAR DIARY
or
INTELLIGENCE SUMMARY.
(Erase heading not required.)

5TH CAVALRY
SUPPLY COLUMN.

Instructions regarding War Diaries and Intelligence Summaries are contained in F. S. Regs., Part II. and the Staff Manual respectively. Title pages will be prepared in manuscript.

Place	Date	Hour	Summary of Events and Information	Remarks and references to Appendices
LA LOGE (near HESDIN)	1/7/17	mid	Usual routine — Major N.M. HUTTON D.S.O. returned from leave & resumed command.	
	2/7/17	mid	Usual routine — Lieut: - received orders to proceed to pharmacists any type of treatment. Later the afternoon he has been arranged to see whilst on a walk with the officers of Division. Lieut. returned to 9th by truck.	
	3/7/17	Bull	Self — m had 4 winners clients. G.H.Q. Inspectors Lieut. boom — 4th Section obtained. parties were away where two Lieutenant & we still engaged on the job.	
	4/7/17	bar	Usual routine.	
	5/7/17	"	"	
	6/7/17	"	" Rode over very hot & sultry	
	7/7/17	"	"	
	8/7/17	"	" provided lorries (3) for supply to 4 Cavalry Bde }	
	9/7/17	"	" Delivered rations to area between AUXI-LE-CHATEAU & DOULLENS	

Army Form C. 2118.

WAR DIARY
or
INTELLIGENCE SUMMARY.
(Erase heading not required.)

5TH CAVALRY SUPPLY COLUMN.

Place	Date	Hour	Summary of Events and Information	Remarks and references to Appendices
LA LOGE	9th	Fine	"B" Section leaves, after detaching 300 Dismounted Reinforcements, journey down to rail-head uneventful, but to return with the RHQ to "C" Section. Plus provisions to lorries cont. D&D.O.W. also sup. 1 train loaded "D" Section & 1 horse drawn train.	
"	10th	Fair	Heavy rain during the night, his night after rg. "B" Section at CANDAS unloading & will park at CANDAS after delivering.	
VILLERS-CARBONNEL ETRE PIGNY	11th	Fine	Motorcyclists Lewis-cups arrived VILLERS-CARBONNEL	
near PERONNE	12th	"	2nd night. Find of Allies in reserve 3 horses etc others area E of PERONNE	
"	13th	Thirty	Delivering supplies "B" off in afternoon. Radios no issued.	
"	14th	Thick	"B" Section empty	
"	15th	"	do yesterday. "B" return to supplies	
"	16th	Fine	5th New Div Park attached into the next Army HQ Kamych but drawn to "A" Section 5th Cavalry Supply Column	

Army Form C. 2118.

WAR DIARY
of
INTELLIGENCE SUMMARY.
(Erase heading not required.)

Instructions regarding War Diaries and Intelligence Summaries are contained in F. S. Regs., Part II. and the Staff Manual respectively. Title pages will be prepared in manuscript.

[Stamp: 5TH CAVALRY SUPPLY COLUMN.]

Place	Date	Hour	Summary of Events and Information	Remarks and references to Appendices
ETREPIGNY Near PERONNE	17/11	Dull Fine	Moved units.	
"	18/11	Dull-fine	"	
"	19/11	Dull-fine	Quartermasters - in providing 8 lorries per Reg. & D.T.s. to deliver supplies from Dumps at 7:30 daily addition to lorry delivering in the road manner. This suggested revision to 10 double echelon system. D/A supplies in concentration res. (FINS) Received rations at midnight & made early journey to bivouac in SAILLY-SAILLISEL (on PERONNE-BAPAUME Road)	
SAILLY -SAILLISEL	20/11	Dull in morning - rain later.	Moved to bivouac in charge at LA CHAPELLETTE. D/A pushed on & supplies to forward area. Division in action. Advanced D.T. etc at - MARCOING.	
"	21/11	Dull-cold	Loaded to send Ord. Gun Amm at YTRES to lagu co railway for advance to MARCOING. Sent 15 wri thre -10 x other kinds. 5 3/4 wo go great. Loaded w/s remainder of supplies at YTRES.	
"	22/11	Dull-fine	Loaded at YTRES & delivered supplies to Adv. transportation. Division returned that return.	
"	23/11	Dull-fine	Loaded at YTRES delivered at 11 am & 4 pm to Dumps by SUSANNE in... Received orders to move column to PROYART	

(A7092). Wt. W12839/M1293. 75,000. 1/17. D. D. & L., Ltd. Forms/C2118-14.

Army Form C. 2118.

WAR DIARY
or
INTELLIGENCE SUMMARY.
(Erase heading not required.)

5TH CAVALRY
SUPPLY COLUMN.
No..................
Date................

Instructions regarding War Diaries and Intelligence Summaries are contained in F. S. Regs., Part II. and the Staff Manual respectively. Title pages will be prepared in manuscript.

Place	Date	Hour	Summary of Events and Information	Remarks and references to Appendices
PROYART	24/7	—	Dull - fine :- Moved to PROYART. Lorry delivery in bulk as usual	
	25/7	—	" — not in convoy.	
	26/7	—	Fine — routine as usual	
	27/7	—	Fine — "	
ESTREES-en-CHAUSSEE.	28/7	—	Fine — moved temporarily material place & convoy yards reconstruction in NISSEN Huts - lorries parked in yards of main road in mud. no protection.	
	29/7	—	Fine — Received orders for "A" section (Ex 2nd this div Pk) to proceed to LA CHAPELLETTE - VILLERS CARBONNEL Rd. & there at disp. Parks of 1st 3rd 4th 5th Can Divisions in lieu of continued "A" section under re Cav Corps through present 91 supplies Rail Head around MONCHY LAGACHE — BRIE.	
	30/7	Fine	Loaded for BRIE - received orders to deliver supplies to B Echelons only. 8 lorries to units (including "A" Lect 2nd Can Pk) 827 all units leaving men up at 9 am to GEUDECOURT. Area is reported the enemy has broken through. "A" Echelon supplies all up	

V. Martin
MAJOR
O. C. 5TH CAV. SUPPLY COL.

WAR DIARY or **INTELLIGENCE SUMMARY**.

Army Form C. 2118.

8th Camp Suff. Regt.

December 1917.

Place	Date	Hour	Summary of Events and Information	Remarks
FRAMERVILLE (near PROYART)	1/12/17	2 am 2 am	Proceeded to march at 2 am to rest on flags at MONCHY-LAGACHE to ATHIES. Received orders re billeting Framerville.	
		6 pm 8 pm	Moved from ESTREES to FRAMERVILLE. Several units and billets accommodation. Hated at LA CHAPELLETTE only B Billion applied going on gross roofs for A. & B.	
	3/12/17 8.30		Hated at LA FLAQUE. Received 35 horses for running to tents, field kitchens, Cooks' Division. Arrived trucks. Train A second transport at supplies at 1 pm. 2 hours reached about heron. From 6 am to 10 am many B & C actually sent sick. Fixed-arr hated at LA FLAQUE at 8.30 am experienced great difficulty day in obtaining orders for delivery of supplies.	
	4/12/17		Fog very - began at day-break at LA FLAQUE & 1 am. — All supplies to brigade forward MONCHY-LAGACHE. 10 am Lorries were afterwards started by motor lambonts to convey troops up the line, not all out were taking to camp until the morning of 5th inst at railway hours between	

(A7092) Wt. W12839/M/493. 75:000. 1/17. D. D. & L. Ltd. Forms/C.2118/14

Army Form C. 2118.

WAR DIARY
or
INTELLIGENCE SUMMARY.
(Erase heading not required.)

Instructions regarding War Diaries and Intelligence Summaries are contained in F. S. Regs., Part II. and the Staff Manual respectively. Title pages will be prepared in manuscript.

Place	Date	Hour	Summary of Events and Information	Remarks and references to Appendices
FRAMERVILLE	5/12/17		Fine & sunny – freezing all day – Had first hot meal. 1/2 Bath all returns at 9 & 10 a.m. "G" Coy buries dead at LA FLAQUE yesterday morning returned the company, looked for lorries again demanded for at 9.30 a.m.	
	6/12/17		Coy rep hopes dry, with off by Complin. Fine sunny - freezing. Loading as thing is yesterday. like bodies to lorries but to dead – 1 L.Cpl. out by my umerraging Lieut – 22 hours and a other	
	7/12/17		Kaite Dull – thaw all day. Routine as yesterday. First civilians the company in 1 L.G.O.C. stale last.	
BIVOUACS ON LA CHAPELLETTE – ETREPIGNY first	8/12/17		Dull - wet later – moved to our usually wintered places, with no exception of dunkelyes Eloie, this received at FRAMERVILLE. Loaded at LA CHAPELLETTE	
	9/12/17		Wet – Thus labour and its question last night. Supplies delivered by three transport. Our troops in billets have by lorries from Peilhel	
	10/12/17		As yesterday. Thaw restriction eased at 6pm tonight	

Army Form C. 2118.

WAR DIARY
or
INTELLIGENCE SUMMARY.
(Erase heading not required.)

Instructions regarding War Diaries and Intelligence Summaries are contained in F.S. Regs., Part II. and the Staff Manual respectively. Title pages will be prepared in manuscript.

Place	Date	Hour	Summary of Events and Information	Remarks and references to Appendices
LA CHAPELLETTE	11/2/17		Twelve dis hit cell. Loading delivery by double collar still.	
	12/2/17		Horsed. 3 horses attached from 93 bg det lent to supply III R.H.A Bde train lines night - day usual water. to be	
			attached VI Corps by supply. Lifted M.G. Squadrons.	
			Routine as usual.	
	13/2/17		Dull - waters as usual	
	14/2/17		Dull - wet. 5 3/4" lorries attached for supplying 311½ Arty Bde.	
	15/2/17		Fog - cold - usual routine. Sleigh platoon attached to "A" Echelon	
			echo, including R.H.A gunners. 640 all	
	16/2/17		Fine - cold - frost hard night - usual routine. Bivs & lorry	
	17/2/17		to BOURSEVILLE 311½ Artillery Bde. 8 additional lorries reported	
			from AULT. Heavy fall snow last night. - usual routine. 14 lorries yoked	
			to return to park tho exceptionally heavy	
			enroute new ESTREES-EN-CHAUSSEE. The rail sheds supplied	
			ten to thirteen lorries - lorries at a failure on	
			practice knop (?) the restraining plates breaking & (2) the	
			cross tie - bolt sheet stripping.	
	18/2/17	11 am	Fine - cold. heavy snow last night - do to 14 lorries mentioned above	

Army Form C. 2118.

WAR DIARY
or
INTELLIGENCE SUMMARY.
(Erase heading not required.)

Instructions regarding War Diaries and Intelligence Summaries are contained in F. S. Regs., Part II. and the Staff Manual respectively. Title pages will be prepared in manuscript.

Place	Date	Hour	Summary of Events and Information	Remarks and references to Appendices
LA CHAPELLETTE	18/7/17	11 am	Have not yet returned.	
			Missing yet their records to me leaves again you leaving	
			the train	
	19/7/17	10—	Onward train not yet retired	
		—	Roll-line — as yesterday. Train returned	
			today. Routine occurred.	
	20/7/17	—	Roll-line — Last retired wounded. Horses which we saddened	
			hours of picking up Iron Ration & reserve of Oats	
			from the Division in mid of this where losing up	
			operation.	
	21/7/17		Roll-line — Loading & delivering in single echelon ("B")	
			"B" Section expect on extraneous duties you the line	
			horses.	
	22/7/17		Roll-line — as yesterday — strength turns 640 all ranks	
	23/7/17		Roll-line — routine normal — provided 19 horses for	
			extraneous duties you the local corps. Last casualties — MIL—	
	24/7/17		NIL — entirely cold during transport — experienced great	

WAR DIARY
or
INTELLIGENCE SUMMARY.

Army Form C. 2118.

Place	Date	Hour	Summary of Events and Information	Remarks and references to Appendices
LA CHAPELLETTE	24/12/17		difficulty in starting engine in consequence. "C" Coy. other others marched 15 for various duties with the lines.	
			12 good arrived. 15 for entraining duties with the lorries. Then sat in shaft till 11 am, but eased during afternoon + there were consequently performed by the troops for leave.	
	25/12/17		D4 heave. Fine - mild + cheering. Our orders to move into [?] at 6pm this evening. Lads arrived [?] Lettres 35 have for entraining + unloading kitbags. Meir XMAS dinner in the evening. Good + plenty vegetables, the ootens performed is absolutely on account of Later :- two night thing yard [?] men.	
	26/12/17		Fine mild - heavy by the roller [?] morning. - Routine covered	
	27/12/17		Fine - cold. - Routine as usual.	
	28/12/17		Fine - cold. thawing as yesterday. Ordered to move at 1.30pm and proceed to billets that 2 Kelly lorries at ESTREES - BOUVINCOURT Road.	

WAR DIARY
or
INTELLIGENCE SUMMARY.
(Erase heading not required.)

Army Form C. 2118.

Place	Date	Hour	Summary of Events and Information	Remarks and references to Appendices
LA CHAPEL LETTE	29/12/17		Fine - cold. Routine.	
	30/12/17		" " Capt. A. THIERSCH proceeded to CHAULNES No 41 Stn. Also at GAILLY, supplying gun mantles & with us to ESTREES.	
ESTREES-en-CHAUSSEE	31/12/17		" " moved to ESTREES, where we are billeted in NISSEN Huts. Main workshops still billeted at FRAMERVILLE - hr. and to finish its not to be taken in several days time. Strength of unit = 696 all ranks.	

VMahler
O.C. 5TH CAV. SUPPLY COL.
MAJOR

5TH CAVALRY
SUPPLY COLUMN.
No.
Date 1-1-18

Army Form C. 2118.

5TH CAVALRY SUPPLY COLUMN.

M.............
Date.............

WAR DIARY or INTELLIGENCE SUMMARY.
(Erase heading not required.)

January 1918

Place	Date	Hour	Summary of Events and Information	Remarks and references to Appendices
ESTREES-EN-CHAUSSÉE	1/1/18		Fine - milder - usual routine	
	2/1/18		Fine - thaw all in, but otherwise temperature dropped quickly, nothing of importance to report.	
	3/1/18		Fine - colder. Attended C.T.C. on accident to Lcr N°. 145'36 (Fairfield - at 306 Laundries Pk. Shae circular, motorcycle at 61. fld. Radio - usual.	
	4/18			
	5/1/18		Fine - told again - routine as usual. Reports yesterdays 'usual run'.	
	6/1/18		Fine - milder - usual routine. Over 29 lorries opt. to road today due to puncture near repair se. Percentage has been very high lately. Returned authority & evacuate Fairfield lor N°. 25823 (1.1.0. lor) circumstance of accident. Thaw set in at about 8 p.m.	
	7/1/18		wet, very mild - thawing rapidly - usual routine. The scheme kept into operation to 9 p.m. this evening - his drivers cancelled late evening - Heavy fall of snow after light frost last night. Routine as usual.	
	8/1/18			

Army Form C. 2118.

WAR DIARY
or
INTELLIGENCE SUMMARY.
(Erase heading not required.)

5TH CAVALRY SUPPLY COLUMN

Place	Date	Hour	Summary of Events and Information	Remarks and references to Appendices
ESTREES- -EN-CHAUSSEE	9th		Many good troop nights returned during the night. Enemy aeroplanes came over with sixty men. Thin aid in cloud 8 P.M.	
	10th		Mild — then continued during night. Routine as usual.	
	11th		Mild — continue the same yesterday. Ration exchange duties. "B" Section today ad 41 supplies to Section requiring intravenous panicked 12 horses today.	
	12th		This scheme commenced at midnight 11/12th and Well — to horses on the rail today. Received Group notification 9 a.m. low Div. 10 K T. No Section stable of Flight put I was very long day. operation.	
	8th		Toddling quad burg the night — act! Long order quad two to Divisional School to BUSS all unloll resumed accupied making very darkings out splinter proof protection around late of rural. ACCB M papers signed MO BRUCE Oak LC.B. returned case to	

WAR DIARY or INTELLIGENCE SUMMARY.

Army Form C. 2118.

5TH CAVALRY SUPPLY COLUMN.

(Erase heading not required.)

Instructions regarding War Diaries and Intelligence Summaries are contained in F.S. Regs., Part II. and the Staff Manual respectively. Title pages will be prepared in manuscript.

Place	Date	Hour	Summary of Events and Information	Remarks and references to Appendices
ESTREES en C.	13th		Still no reply. Drew up large & distributed to perso.	
	"	9.45 p.m.	The instructions excelled Convoi but Relieve supplies to next scenario ("B" section)	
	14th		First day right, but blend rapidly this received instructions to have all personnel medically suited "A" to "B". Turning to "B" no known officer brakesman together expected. Issued 14th to B's reserve "their relieve" turnpo, no rail dep supply of gauge will supplied the scenario.	
	15th		"B" letting held delivered supplies. The scheme came into position. All Personnel medically examined graded either "A" or "B".	
	16th	6 p.m.	Mid. — No lorries running. Supplies held up by H.T. All open preserved engaged in making protection of entrenches around huts.	
	17th		Mid. — nil. so yesterday.	
	18th		Mid. — nil. The scheme to continue in operation.	
	19th		yes 16th and 19th int. A men in units = 194) detail only B " " " = 147) personnel only	

Army Form C. 2118.

5TH CAVALRY SUPPLY COLUMN.
No. ....
Date. ....

WAR DIARY or INTELLIGENCE SUMMARY.
(Erase heading not required.)

Instructions regarding War Diaries and Intelligence Summaries are contained in F. S. Regs., Part II. and the Staff Manual respectively. Title pages will be prepared in manuscript.

Place	Date	Hour	Summary of Events and Information
ESTREES en - C.	20/7/18		Sunday – nothing to report
	21/7/18		Wet – then "restrictive" rendered cart & bpd. Roads in very bad condition
	22/7/18		Wet – wet – "b" Echelon on supplies – "B" Echelon on ordnance duties. All available spare lorries conveyed to Lihyo "dumpo" Garage repair dept. Rushed to Bde. Recent depôt (1 for Evans) in no event of the restriction being again required.
	23/7/18		Mild days – usual routine on supplies and retrieving hills. 4 placed at S.B.M. q. "B" Echelon with escort of hay, drunk with corps. Remains to be m/t gave emerging entrance – no yesterday
	24/7/18		Officer not had by O.C. A.S.C
	25/7/18		Fine – mild – usual routine. Formerly claim for 100 litres officer – rate by mod individuals for relief damage to gun at present accepted by a gun previously used by the French - Paravane kilt by m/Z german. Long m to wm gradual dismissed

(A7092) Wt. W2839/M1293. 75,000. 1/17. D. D. & L., Ltd. Forms/C2118/14.

Army Form C. 2118.

5TH CAVALRY SUPPLY COLUMN.

No.
Date.

WAR DIARY
or
INTELLIGENCE SUMMARY.
(Erase heading not required.)

Instructions regarding War Diaries and Intelligence Summaries are contained in F. S. Regs., Part II. and the Staff Manual respectively. Title pages will be prepared in manuscript.

Place	Date	Hour	Summary of Events and Information	Remarks and references to Appendices
ESTRÉES en-CHAUSSÉE	26/2		Fine, windy. Usual routine. Received Preliminary instructions re move to DOMART on 28/30th & DOMART area. (2 copy)	
	27/2		Fine – issued instructions re issuing supplies to Divn Qrs. on 28th & 29th Feb. ALSO arrangements re moves, billets & rns at HALLOY (SOMME) on 29/2/20th. Usual routine.	
	28/2		Fine, cooler – usual routine. Yesterday taken brevet rly. Had two prisoners en route brevet rly. All arrived safely.	
HALLOY (SOMME)	29/2		Fine – went to HALLOY – newly appointed.	
	30/2		Fine – "B" Echelon routed via Mignes, Berneuil, 16th Echelon to CANDAS.	
	31/2		Fine – cooler – "B" Echelon halted at CANDAS – "D" Echelon moved & billeted in HALLOY – killed in the district Workshops in CANAPLES. Strength of unit – 107, all ranks (admin includes M.T. personnel employed as "A" Ech during).	

Army Form C. 2118.

WAR DIARY
or
INTELLIGENCE SUMMARY.
(Erase heading not required.)

Instructions regarding War Diaries and Intelligence Summaries are contained in F. S. Regs., Part II. and the Staff Manual respectively. Title pages will be prepared in manuscript.

Place	Date	Hour	Summary of Events and Information	Remarks and references to Appendices
HALLOY to PERNOIS	3/1/17		Our entire march in excellent weather. Our route lay up the railway line Halloy - Doullens. Travelled the first nettable road from hereabout. Transport vehicles in good condition to interval which kept as laid-down in an invariably then observed.	

[Stamp: 5TH CAVALRY SUPPLY COLUMN. No...... Date......]

[Stamp: 5TH CAVALRY SUPPLY COLUMN. No. 1 Date 2-18]

J. Mahner
MAJOR
O.C. 5th CAV. SUPPLY COL.

WAR DIARY
or
INTELLIGENCE SUMMARY.

(Erase heading not required.)

Army Form C. 2118.

5TH CAVALRY SUPPLY COLUMN.

Place	Date	Hour	Summary of Events and Information	Remarks and references to Appendices
HALLOY- PERNOIS	1/8/18	Fine	Received instructions to select 5 G.S. limbers at 5 L.g.G.S. to accompany 4th Cav. Bay. Column to Pernois to report.	G.H.C. G.F.C.
	2/8/18	Wet	Company experiencing some difficulty in obtaining ?	
	3/8/18	Fine	"A" Section owing to their being rail a failure.	G.F.C.
	4/8/18	any	Fine - about to be selected.	
	5/8/18	Fine	and routine.	
			2 cars - selected 28 drivers to accompany vehicles received selected for nine great & selected gun park to transfer to Cav.	G.F.C.
	6/8/18	Journey		
	7/8/18	Fine	- routine received.	G.F.C.
			- " " - received 28 here received	
	8/8/18	but	you men proceeding review.	G.F.C.
		wet	- and routine - received instructions to supply 4 b... ... in ...	
			LONGPRE Cav. Division from 10th inst.	G.F.C.
LONGPRE- le-Corps- Saints	9/8/18	Fine	Moved Column to LONGPRE - Distribution Left here shortly filled. Here an emergency experienced difficulty in obtaining superior revelation. The unit was promised ... ... which either being great ... ... carried.	G.F.C.

August 11th Nov. 1915

WAR DIARY
or
INTELLIGENCE SUMMARY
(Erase heading not required.)

Army Form

5TH CAVALRY SUPPLY COLUMN.

Instructions regarding War Diaries and Intelligence Summaries are contained in F.S. Regs., Part II. and the Staff Manual respectively. Title Pages will be prepared in manuscript.

Place	Date	Hour	Summary of Events and Information	Remarks and references to Appendices
LONGPRÉ les Corps-Saints	10/7/18		Fine – held Sections held at LONGPRÉ "B" to 4th Div. Divs who are lately billeted on this side only.	Delivery 4/h
			AMIENS. Very long run columns, especially anything the right route party to Div of 3rd Division of 5th Div Divs (Res.) in charge, arrived to present.	
	11/7/18		Fine – wind – no yesterday.	
	12/7/18		Fine – received 7 lorries from 4th Dec Erpl. (S. – L.G.O.C.) and 2 C.B. Daimlers) in exchange for 6 C.B. Daimlers and 1 L.G.O.C. from here. The remaining 7 lorries from 4th D.S.C. will be sent later.	
	13/7/18		Wet – usual routine.	
	14/7/18		Instr = received morning lorries from 4th bodybelt. lorries received from 4th Div. are in very poor condition and in need of extensive repair.	
	15/7/18 16/7/18		Wet – usual routine.	
			Fine = elet – everybody. Lorries all the way to the Div are carrying troops than their full military load. Wind cloudy fat out military.	
	17/7/18		Fine – within Today evening the 4th Div output lorries arrived was the 4th Div output.	

2449 Wt. W14957/M90 750,000 1/16 J.B.C. & A. Forms/C.2118/12.

WAR DIARY
or
INTELLIGENCE SUMMARY

(Erase heading not required.)

Army Form

9TH CAVALRY SUPPLY COLUMN

Place	Date	Hour	Summary of Events and Information	Remarks and references to Appendices
LONGPRÉ 1. C. 5.	18/3/18		Fine + mild - were sent for supply - sent 18 mil quality of GN2. a report to Lotters at ROSIERES. Letters at recent. 5th Army School 3/3" Jany Drury GN2 at recent. 19" below today of	
"	19/3/18		SALEUEL LONGPRÉ at 4" Gen Hos Capt HATHIERSEN (wounded) [illegible] hs&s requires stam ability. Fire drill as yesterday. Letters recd as yesterday.	GN2
	20/3/18		4 men over 38 yrs of age who are recommended for Anne Duties under S.S Army Rro 1956. Fine + healthy - recent precautionary orders re Chon	GN2
	21/3/18		the loss of enemy info received under No 12 lorries from 4½ Div. ambulance Convex large lorries in fairly good condition for wild - routine work. submitted line return. 176 men reported this week sick leave. Received instructions from GN2 2nd Lt R Linaskie 2nd Lt J DRURY to 1st Sqn Supol (Arm Ser). 2nd Lt VM HALL. 2 in charge Yr ? 2nd Lt. Brown in w order to enable Sgt DRURY to proceed overseas only 2nd Lieut Regt of 4½ + 5½ Gen Division. The instructions received from a circular as above Yr the same purpose to 2/Lt R.T. GORTON (2d. O. 9th Gun Suplol) with Lt. E.P. PEARCE.	

2449 Wt. W14957/M90 750,000 1/16 J.B.C. & A. Forms/C.2118/12.

WAR DIARY
or
INTELLIGENCE SUMMARY
(Erase heading not required.)

Army Form C. 2118.

Place	Date	Hour	Summary of Events and Information	Remarks and references to Appendices
LONGPRÉ les-Corps Saints	23rd		Dull, gusty. Held routine as usual.	
	24th		Fine — usual routine	
	25th		"	
	26th		Capt. J.R. Gordon transferred to 4th Can. Div. Supply Column. Lt. Pearce joined this unit.	
	27th		Raining. Routine as usual. Major V.M. HUTTON proceeded to 4th Can. Inf. Div. Supply Column.	
	28th		Dull, with rain. Retired T. Davis & 4 men transferred to this unit. Lt. Col. CHAPLIN (CASC) assumed command.	
	29th		Fine — 7th Dragoon Guards marched out, their billets being taken over by 11th Hussars.	
	30th		Stronger Column (all ranks) 709 including 62 drivers attached to Div. troops & Divisional units. Horses — good.	

signed G.P. Chaplin
Major
O.C. 5th Cav. Supply Col.

www.ingramcontent.com/pod-product-compliance
Lightning Source LLC
Chambersburg PA
CBHW081554160426
43191CB00011B/1926